The life of Mozart

Musical lives

The books in this series will each consider
an account of the life of a major composer,
considering both the private and the public
figure. The main thread will be biographical,
and discussion of the music will be integral
to the narrative. Each book thus presents an
organic view of the composer, the music,
and the circumstances in which the music
was written.

Published titles

The life of Bellini JOHN ROSSELLI

The life of Debussy ROGER NICHOLS

The life of Mahler PETER FRANKLIN

The life of Mozart JOHN ROSSELLI

The life of Webern KATHRYN BAILEY

The life of Mozart

JOHN ROSSELLI

CAMBRIDGE
UNIVERSITY PRESS

b. & T.   B / Mozart   14.95

3/99

PUBLISHED BY THE PRESS SYNDICATE OF THE UNIVERSITY OF CAMBRIDGE
The Pitt Building, Trumpington Street, Cambridge CB2 1RP, United Kingdom

CAMBRIDGE UNIVERSITY PRESS
The Edinburgh Building, Cambridge, CB2 2RU, United Kingdom
40 West 20th Street, New York, NY 10011-4211, USA
10 Stamford Road, Oakleigh, Melbourne 3166, Australia

First published 1998

Printed in the United Kingdom at the University Press, Cambridge

Typeset in FF Quadraat 9.75/14 pt, in QuarkXPress™ [SE]

A catalogue record for this book is available from the British Library

Library of Congress cataloguing in publication data

Rosselli, John.
The life of Mozart / by John Rosselli.
     p.   cm. – (Musical lives)
Includes bibliographical references and index.
ISBN 0 521 58317 9 (hardback) – ISBN 0 521 58744 1 (paperback)
1. Mozart, Wolfgang Amadeus, 1756–1791.   2. Composers – Austria –
Biography.   I. Title.   II. Series.
ML410.M9R847   1998
780'.92–dc21

To Lisa
'*Voi che sapete* . . .'

CONTENTS

ILLUSTRATIONS

ix

What follows is a short critical biography of Mozart, designed to place his life and music in their historical context, and based on the vast amount of material available in print. The principles on which it is structured are set out in the Introduction.

I am not a musicologist but an historian with a strong interest in music and a lifelong devotion to Mozart's work. When faced with questions of evidence, historians are apt to say rather often 'we do not know' or 'the evidence is not such as to make possible a firm conclusion'. Readers will find a number of such statements about aspects of Mozart's life. They should at least make a change from some recent biographies. On the interpretation of Mozart's music I have not hesitated to quote from works of criticism where they make a point better than I could.

Titles of operas are given in the form most familiar in English-speaking countries – The Marriage of Figaro, but La clemenza di Tito – and Köchel catalogue numbers in the traditional rather than the revised form, which is still unfamiliar to most people. Quotations from the letters of Wolfgang, Leopold, and Anna Maria Mozart are taken from The Letters of Mozart and his Family, translated by Emily Anderson (3rd revised edn, London, 1985). Quotations from other contemporary documents are mostly taken from O. E. Deutsch, ed., Mozart: A Documentary Biography (London, 1965), and C. Eisen, ed., New Mozart Documents (London, 1991). The sources of other quotations can be found by consulting the note on further reading at the end of the book (pp. 163–6).

Sums of money are given in florins (also known as gulden). The Vienna florin was worth about 8 to 9 to the pound sterling, but both prices and wages were generally much lower in the Austrian lands than in Britain. The Salzburg florin was worth about five-sixths of the Vienna florin.

Part of the discussion of *Così fan tutte* in Chapter 4 first appeared, in somewhat different form, in *The Times Literary Supplement* of 7 June 1991.

Introduction: on the cusp

On 26 January 1790 a new opera had its first performance at the chief Vienna theatre. Its title, hit upon at the last moment, might be rendered as *Girls Will Play*; more literally, as *Women All Behave Like That*. Its subtitle, *The School for Lovers*, showed that it belonged to a long-standing popular genre, Italian comic opera. This dealt, in sung exchanges as a rule light, graceful, speedy, with the more obvious foibles of humankind: just now, with the absurdity of expecting faithfulness in women – shown in a tale of two men each of whom, farcically disguised, wins over the other's 'inconsolable' lover within twenty-four hours of having – it seems – left for the front. Musicians and librettists had churned out such works for the previous half-century; *Così fan tutte* drew for its situations on many of them, though with flourishes from more august literary sources – as, in the cinema, a Western draws on familiar skies and conflicts though from a new, would-be serious angle.

The new work did well enough – not as well as some by proper Italian composers (one of whom had turned down the libretto after sketching out a scene or two), but respectably. The monarch, the Emperor Joseph II, was too ill to attend; his death on 20 February would interrupt the run after ten performances. Another operagoer, a nobleman who kept a diary, noted that the subject was 'rather amusing'; 'the music by Mozart is charming ...'

Emperor and nobleman – and Mozart – had reason to think of events far beyond the opera, the theatre, or Vienna itself. In France, where Joseph II's sister Marie-Antoinette was queen, the Bastille had fallen on 14 July 1789, six and a half months before the first performance of *Così fan tutte*. Then had come the Declaration of the Rights of Man and Citizen, the renunciation of feudal privileges; in October the mob had forced the king and queen from Versailles back into Paris. The dissolution of monastic orders was to come within the next few months, as was that of nobility itself. But although the most drastic changes still lay a short way ahead, in Vienna as in other European cities educated people knew that the French Revolution was transforming the order of things.

An 'enlightened', reforming sovereign like Joseph might have welcomed some of the changes; he could not welcome the popular agitation – running into violence – that had brought them about. His deliberately plain clothes and manner did not mean that he would wish to see aristocracy done away with and the 'middling' people (or Third Estate) set up as master. To the jobbing composer Wolfgang Amadé Mozart, on the other hand (himself apt to feel he must have a 'beautiful red coat' to set off some mother-of-pearl and topaz buttons), the rise of the Third Estate answered a long-frustrated wish. He had suffered through the hauteur and thoughtlessness of those he sometimes caricatured as 'Duchess Smackbottom' or 'Princess Dunghill'; a count in the service of a prince-archbishop had once literally kicked him out, foot landed square on his behind. 'It is the heart', Mozart once wrote, 'that ennobles man' – a commonplace at the time among the forward-looking, but he meant it. The French Revolution from the start raised the cry 'the career open to talent', wonderful to the ears of the unprivileged young. Mozart – just thirty-four at the time of *Così fan tutte* – knew he could compose better than any of his rivals, Haydn alone excepted; yet he had again and again seen others land an established post while he was left unbeneficed. For him the 'opening to talent' could not come too soon.

Così fan tutte might look like just another Italian comic opera. It was in fact a token of a world on the cusp of change. Mozart's most perfect dramatic work enshrines a society where men and women need concern themselves only with delectable follies, and where reconciliation mends all in the name of sense. Music of ideal beauty lifts the ironies of the tale onto a plane of grace – but that grace, as Scott Burnham has written, is 'fugitive, transitory . . . a glimpse of a paradise now discerned as an illusory realm forever beyond the pale of mundane reality yet somehow still true'. The ambience of *Così fan tutte* is what the ex-revolutionary Talleyrand meant when, in old age, he remarked that only those who had grown up before 1789 could know the sweetness of life. Afterwards came struggle and earnestness. *Così fan tutte* is the fine flower of the old regime at its point of dissolution.

Mozart's life as much as his art shows him on the cusp of change from the old world to the new. His early career as child prodigy depended on the favour of monarchs, petty princes, and nobles; in adolescence and early youth he had to work for a ruler who seated him just above the cooks; even as an independent concert artist and composer in Vienna he had to play to a limited audience, still heavily aristocratic, apt to get bored and look elsewhere. Though he sought the dignity of a free artist he just missed, through early death, the conditions that would give a free artist the chance of a wider public and a less troubled career.

Again, he lived at a time when composers expected to turn out music for everyday use, one piece after another as the need arose – whether a special commission or a regular duty, like J. S. Bach's 199 church cantatas or Haydn's more than one hundred trios for his noble patron to play on the obsolescent baryton, a kind of viola da gamba. Mozart too wrote his share of serenades, masses, or German dances to order; he did not pursue a musical idea beyond a sketched beginning if he saw no likelihood of its being performed. Yet impatience of patronage led him more than once to leave a bespoke series unfinished, and he again and again burst the accustomed bounds of a genre – of comic opera with *Don Giovanni*, of the symphony with his last four, of serenade and chamber music with several works that did not readily fit into the musical life of the time; in his piano concertos he virtually invented a new genre.

1   Mozart in his thirties: unfinished oil painting by his brother-in-law the
actor–painter Joseph Lange. Though perhaps slightly idealised, this is one
of the few portraits to give a sense of the eager creative artist.

Though often called a traditionalist who took the musical language
of his day as he found it, he – together with Haydn – changed it so pervasively as to make for a new emotional relationship between music
and its audience; as master of delicately calibrated shifts in harmony
he made music speak to and for inner feeling with a varied eloquence
no one before him had attained. Music had been for use, for community, for religious contemplation, for pleasure, for a connoisseur's

interest in minor new departures; after Mozart it was for life, for love, for the shadow of death, for the individual's profoundest experiences. Most crucially, Mozart lived in a time of transition from a Europe where the community believed unhesitatingly in a spiritual world not theirs to one where the individual would live on his or her own resources; he bridged – we might say – the Christian and post-Christian eras. He himself always wrote straightforwardly that he relied on God and looked forward to meeting the people he loved in a better world; yet some of his last works open out on a secular humanism. In *The Magic Flute*, in the tiny motet 'Ave, verum corpus', truth speaks in human voices without a hint of an overarching power.

In a remarkable passage written between the two world wars of our own century, the theologian Karl Barth claimed Mozart's music as the true Christian's 'food and drink' because Mozart was not a 'self' frantic to express itself but a unique 'ear' open to the music of creation:

> he heard the harmony of creation in which the shadow also belongs but in which the shadow is not darkness, deficiency is not defeat, sadness cannot become despair, trouble cannot degenerate into tragedy and infinite melancholy is not ultimately forced to claim undisputed sway. Thus the cheerfulness in this harmony is not without its limits. But the light shines all the more brightly because it breaks forth from the shadow ... Mozart saw this light no more than we do, but he heard the whole world of creation enveloped by this light.

Mozart's music, according to Barth, showed that although creation included a Yes and a No it was not disordered, not cleft between God and nothingness; even in its No, hence as a totality, 'creation praises its Master and is therefore perfect.'

Barth used to listen to some Mozart every day, in effect as to an angel – a messenger of God. Many people, it seems likely, hear as Barth did. Unbelievers though most of them probably are, in this music they glimpse the spirit – 'airs from heaven and blasts from hell', as Bernard Shaw wrote of *Don Giovanni*, reconciled in a work of art that brings peace.

Barth's, however, is not the only Mozart. Writers on the Marxist Left have been at pains to bring out the Mozart who played an active part in the 'enlightened' movements of his time, Freemasonry in particular, and who in his resentment of the aristocracy and upper clergy anticipated the supposedly bourgeois revolution of 1789. Those of more conservative outlook tend to play down Mozart's political engagement and interpret his works accordingly. Vast audiences exposed to Peter Shaffer's *Amadeus* – play and film – harbour the image of Mozart as a lout who is also an inspired artist. Biographers involve themselves in Mozart's two chief personal relationships – with his father and his wife; some take sides, at times relying heavily on speculation or on what they think modern psychoanalysis can tell us about eighteenth-century motives.

The present work rests as far as possible on Mozart's own documentation – his letters, together with those of his father – and on the more reliable other documents of the time, set within the context of their society. Though it is bound to look into Mozart's relationships it seeks to avoid guesswork. In trying to understand Mozart we none the less face difficulties. His surviving letters are many and tell us a great deal, yet they are most of them addressed to members of his family; in writing to his father in particular – perhaps at times to his wife – Mozart, it has become clear, was not always truthful. If we had more letters to friends and fellow artists we might get a different impression. For much of 1773–77 and 1779–80 – when all the family were in Salzburg and need not write – again after Wolfgang's break with Salzburg in 1781, still more after his father's death in 1787, the correspondence slackens or disappears; in some years we have little evidence.

More fundamentally, what matters to us in this fellow human being is his music. The present study takes the work as no less central to its inquiry than the life; indeed it assumes that the chief events in that life, one or two apart, were musical. Mozart's compositions, however, run into hundreds: a short book cannot begin to deal with them all. The following chapters dwell on certain works as particularly significant;

others they ignore or deal with as categories and groups. The significant works do not always appear in chronological order. Once Mozart had achieved his mature style – when he was about eighteen – he did not in any obvious sense 'progress' from work to work; at most we may ask whether the last year or two of his life show the coming of a 'late style' that might reflect changes in his personal and artistic outlook. A work of his mature period may therefore legitimately be taken out of order to illustrate a theme in what he still says to us.

For all these reasons Chapters 1 and 2 deal with Mozart's childhood and youth and his emancipation from authority, Chapter 3 with his marriage and with the music of the early Vienna period, the piano concertos especially. Chapters 4 and 5 follow two themes across Mozart's major phase, his involvement with opera and his inmost beliefs as they are reflected in his works. Chapter 6 deals with his 'late' phase, Chapter 7 with his illness and death.

At the core of what Mozart says to us lies something that cannot be taken to bits and explained. After repeated hearings, its mystery endures. That is why we go on listening to it. Having listened, we must in the end leave some questions open.

1 Escape from the father

'All the ladies are in love with my boy', Leopold Mozart reported from Vienna in October 1762. The boy was six, some of the ladies very great ladies indeed: the Empress Maria Theresia spent three hours at her Schönbrunn palace with the Mozart family, during which little Woferl not only played the harpsichord but 'jumped up on the empress's lap, put his arms round her neck and kissed her heartily'. At Versailles over a year later the royal princesses kissed the boy as he went by; Queen Marie Leszczynska fed him from dishes on her table, but this time he stood and merely kissed her hands over and over. Later still at Buckingham House the family met Queen Charlotte and George III, so friendly and attentive that a week later in St James's Park, 'although we all had on different clothes', the king leaned out of his carriage and greeted them, 'especially our Master Wolfgang, nodding to us and waving his hand'. Between the ages of six and fourteen, while other boys kept to the daily round of home and, perhaps, school, Mozart toured Europe as a star performer everywhere made much of by the greatest in the land.

The child prodigy as exhibit was something of a novelty. It already made some people shake their heads: such early fruit would yield little later on, and the children would face the disappointment of being, after all, no better than their contemporaries. Many none the less revelled in what Mozart's father Leopold always described as a 'miracle of God', a 'wonder of nature' he was bound to make known to the world, just as many twentieth-century people were to revel in films starring Shirley Temple or the latest four-years-old cinemoppet.

Such a childhood went a long way to shape the grown man's sensibility and outlook, all the more because the way Leopold ran his son's life made – as their letters show – for complex, difficult relations between the two later on. Much of Wolfgang's life up to the age of twenty-five, when he set up as an independent musician, was a prolonged, necessary, in part bungled escape from the father he loved.

The boy was born in his parents' Salzburg flat on 27 January 1756; next day he was baptised in Salzburg Cathedral with the names Joannes Chrysostomus Wolfgangus Theophilus. The birthplace, the town, the names are all significant.

The flat consisted of three rooms, all of them wide but so low-ceilinged as to image the filling in a sandwich. They opened one into the other: the corridor, an eighteenth-century invention, came too late for the builders of the house. No corridor meant no space shut off as a bedroom, no privacy in the modern sense, no setting off of the individual apart from the family. Biographers who misunderstand Wolfgang's relations with his father and sister unconsciously assume that each acted, modern British or American fashion, as one distinct individual facing others. They do not allow for the family, an overarching body all the Mozarts were inescapably part of even when they were angry with one another or were no longer communicating.

Salzburg was a handsome, prosperous town in a part of the German-speaking lands where Roman Catholicism, imposed once again by force after the Reformation, now held sway as the unquestioned, often deeply felt religion. It was the seat of a principality ruled by an archbishop, one of the hundreds of states large and small that made up the Holy Roman Empire – a ramshackle, weak leftover from the Middle Ages, spread over much of central Europe. Contemporaries tended to think of Salzburg as geographically part of Bavaria to the north; Munich, the Bavarian capital, was the nearest large city. To the south, Italy was within easy reach: the town had for over a century employed Italian architects and musicians, and Italian musical influence was strong.

Was not Mozart an Austrian, then? No one thought of Austria as a nation to which Salzburg obviously belonged. The Habsburg dynasty in Vienna ruled over the Austrian hereditary lands, which did not include Salzburg; most of these lands were, like Salzburg, within the Holy Roman Empire, of which the Habsburg ruler was almost automatically the head, and in many the upper classes at least spoke German. The Habsburgs were also kings of Hungary, a large area outside the Empire. In Vienna the Empress Maria Theresia and her husband and children wrote each other little notes in French, German, or Italian as the fancy took them: French was the medium of polite exchange throughout Europe; all three languages were among those spoken by their subjects. They could muster some Hungarian if need be, and in everyday conversation they and their nobles fell into Viennese dialect. Mozart was born into a part of Europe where nationality in the modern sense did not exist.

As he grew up, some educated people – himself among them – talked at times warmly of promoting the German language and German music, but they did not look for a united German state. If Germanness had a capital (which was doubtful) that capital was Vienna, but in Vienna as in Salzburg the educated looked almost as much to France and Italy as to central Europe. Mozart was to dedicate his string quartets to Haydn in Italian (the language of music), and now and then to write to his family in Italian or French.

His baptismal names symbolised these openings to different cultures. The first two names, those of the saint on whose day he was born, marked the family's steadfast Catholic piety. Wolfgang, the name his family chose to call him by, was straightforwardly German. Theophilus ('lover of God') was the Greek form of a name often rendered in Latin as Amadeus, or at times in German as Gottlieb. Mozart himself in later life more often than not signed himself

2 View of Schönbrunn: engraving by Carl Schütz

Wolfgang Amadé – another linguistic hybrid, for the Amadé, a form occasionally met with in German-speaking lands, was a conflation of Amadeus and the French Amédée.

Wolfgang was the last of seven children born to Leopold Mozart and his wife Anna Maria Pertl since their marriage nine years earlier; he and his sister Maria Anna, born five years earlier and usually called Marianne or Nannerl, were the only ones to survive.

Leopold (1719–87) came of a family of artisans – masons, weavers, bookbinders – in Augsburg, not far beyond Munich. His wife, a year younger, was the daughter of a minor official from a town near Salzburg; her relatives included musicians. Leopold had come to music by way of an elaborate Jesuit education, in effect to university level. It mattered to his own and his son's career that he could write well (if sometimes at pedantic length), knew languages ancient and modern, and was trained in philosophy, mathematics, and science. This education was meant to take him into the priesthood, but he dropped out and took a post as musician with a great nobleman, soon followed by one with the prince-archbishop of Salzburg. That he now and then wrote sarcastically about priests – while remaining a devout Catholic – tells us little: many people from Maria Theresia and her son Joseph II on down sought to clear the Church of abuses such as 'idle' monks or priests without thereby departing from their faith.

Leopold was a representative 'enlightened' intellectual of moderate outlook, critical of the privileged but bent on taking the world rationally as he found it; he detested frontal attacks on Catholicism such as Voltaire had launched, and in writing to him his son was to crow over Voltaire's death ('like a dog, like a beast!'). Nor does Leopold's estrangement from his mother (over an inheritance he thought due) necessarily bear the weight that psychoanalytically based biography has placed on it; he remained on good terms with his brother Franz Alois and went to some trouble to keep his citizenship of Augsburg. In 1756, soon after Wolfgang's birth, he brought out a treatise on violin playing that is still well regarded. As a composer he was accomplished but without showing particular originality or moving out of the 'galant' musical language then in use for non-religious music – of short melodic phrases neatly arranged and limpidly orchestrated.

For all his ostentatious knowledge of the world and his genuine shrewdness, Leopold's was a restless spirit, newly inflamed on discovering that he had fathered a 'miracle'. The composer J. A. Hasse, a balanced observer who saw something of him in Vienna, thought him 'equally discontented everywhere'. This could never be said of his wife, an amiable soul, clearly subordinate to her husband. Such is the personality that comes out of her letters; we can make out little more. That she and other members of the family indulged in scatological humour – she once wrote to Leopold 'shit in your bed and make it burst' – means little more than that they shared the manners of the place and time they lived in. Not only Salzburg but other German-speaking lands enjoyed lavatory jokes; for that matter, eighteenth-century British people could be earthier in their intimate correspondence than later censored editions show.

The five children dead in infancy raise the same question as the adult Wolfgang's four (out of six) who were to die within hours or weeks of their birth. How did parents bear it? They grieved – historical evidence suggests – no less because child deaths were common. All the same, for women to live through repeated pregnancies, and for both parents to suffer the death of one child after another when that was the common lot, must have been an experience unlike that of stricken families in modern advanced societies where such things happen very rarely.

If these deaths made the Mozart parents specially protective of their last child we do not know of it. The baby's birth had been difficult. In line with a current theory, they fed him on barley water; the alternative – because breast-feeding was still thought lower-class – would have been a wet-nurse, notoriously liable to expose the child to disease. Wolfgang grew up small – he never attained more than five feet four inches – pale, and none too robust.

As Wolfgang was getting on for four his sister Nannerl began to have keyboard lessons for which her father assembled contemporary pieces. The boy started picking out chords and then learning and play-ing pieces out of his sister's notebook. At five he composed some short keyboard pieces of his own (he still had not learned standard notation); at six he began to teach himself the violin; at seven he took on the organ, though if he sat at the keyboard his feet would not reach the pedals, so he had to play standing up.

He had a teacher at hand – his father. Leopold taught his children not only music theory and instrumental playing but almost every-thing else they ever learnt formally. He did a good job. Besides their music – Nannerl too became a fine pianist – they were fluent in Italian and French, they could cope in Latin, they had a little English (unusual in their day), by adolescence they wrote well (if only let-ters); Wolfgang showed himself keen and able at mathematics; what we can see of their general culture was of a good standard for musi-cians, whose time then as now was engrossed by instrumental prac-tice.

3 Mozart aged about seven, very much the self-concious child prodigy:
oil painting by Pietro Antonio Lorenzoni, 1763

By Wolfgang's sixth year his father knew he had a prodigy to direct.
This was not just his opinion. Nearly everyone who heard Wolfgang
play on the family's European tours was amazed. What amazed them
most, and what made Wolfgang's first reputation, was his ability as a
performer on keyboard and violin, above all as sight-reader and

improviser. The musicologist Charles Burney, who heard him when he was from eight to nine years old, saw him compose a treble to a given bass (and vice versa), improvise and play at sight, finish a composition begun by another, imitate the vocal styles of reigning opera stars in an 'extempore opera to nonsense words', and play a three-movement overture and accompanied recitatives 'all full of taste [and] imagination, with good harmony, melody, and modulation . . .'

The first trip Leopold organised to show off his children was to the court of the Elector of Bavaria at Munich, in January 1762. In September–December they went to Vienna, with halts at or side trips to Passau (seat of another prince-bishop), Linz, and the Hungarian capital, Pressburg (now Bratislava).

The times were favourable: the hard-fought Seven Years War was ending; rulers and nobles had the leisure to enjoy a musical wonder and the money to pay for it. This trip set the pattern of later ones. Leopold aimed chiefly at courts – not only those of kings but of minor German rulers and of local viceroys, like the Habsburg princes in charge of the Austrian Netherlands (now Belgium) and of Milan – because courts were still the centres of power and wealth: he hoped the ruler would pay well for a concert (in money or, a poor second best, in jewellery), though he found more than once that the 'charming' monarchical custom was 'to keep people waiting for presents for a long time'. Besides the ruler, each court afforded noble men and women eager to hear the children, at public concerts or in private. Then there were the self-governing cities like Geneva and Frankfurt, big trade centres like Amsterdam and Lyons, above all the two greatest cities in Europe, London and Paris, where a sizeable, well-off, and fashionable public, some of them musically aware, eclipsed the wealth of the court.

From June 1763 to November 1766 the family engaged in a monster tour of south and west Germany, Belgium, Paris (a five-month stay), London (a fifteen-month stay, no less), Belgium again, Holland (eight months), Paris again, through Burgundy to Geneva and other Swiss cities, then more south German courts on the way home. Further tours ensued, to Vienna (September 1767 – December 1768, with a side trip to Brünn or Brno in Moravia) and to Italy (December 1769 – March 1771), with extended stays in Milan, Florence, Rome, Naples, Bologna, and Venice.

There were to be two further, short Italian tours (August–December 1771 and October 1772 – March 1773) and trips to Vienna (July–September 1773) and Munich (December 1774 – March 1775), but the first Italian tour in 1769–71 marked the end of Wolfgang's time as a prodigy. In the summer of 1770 his voice broke; he was then fourteen. An adolescent player would no longer seem miraculous; a wiseacre would soon write that his compositions showed such 'early fruit' to be 'more extraordinary than excellent'. Besides, just before he entered puberty Wolfgang had contracted to write a serious opera for the royal theatre in Milan – in contemporary eyes, the most notable task a musician could undertake. The opera, *Mitridate*, was a success; the purpose of the later trips to Italy and to Munich was to fulfil similar commissions. Though still known at least as much as a performer, Mozart was now a professional composer.

He had fully earned the name of prodigy. When he was not quite eleven a knowledgeable observer thought he outdid any keyboard player even though his hands were so small that he had to spread an octave. His ear was so keen that he could hear and remember a difference of an eighth of a tone in the tuning of two violins. In London when he was nine and singing a duet at sight he showed 'some anger' at his father's being once or twice out, and put him right. If ever genius was inborn it was in Mozart. But it was a musical genius: only in music did Leopold find that his son knew 'in his eighth year what I would expect only from a man of forty'. Wolfgang's mathematical ability (which often goes with music) may also have been notable, but is too ill documented for us to gauge it.

Life as a prodigy was hard even though it meant being petted by queens and dressing up in a lilac coat with a moiré waistcoat, both

4 Leopold Mozart: oil painting by Pietro Antonio Lorenzoni, 1765. The only
portrait to bring out his blend of the authoritarian and the punctilious.

trimmed with wide gold braid. 'Nothing but dressing and undress-
ing, packing and unpacking', Leopold wrote in an Italian January,
'and withal no warm room, so that one freezes like a dog'; the
thirteen-year-old Wolfgang got chilblains. Many roads were bad;
paved roads were rare. From a nobleman's villa where they slept in

fine linen sheets and washed out of a silver ewer they might find themselves translated to 'horrible, filthy inns'.

The children were more than once seriously ill; they would no doubt have fallen ill at home, but illness on the road was harder to cope with, and the enforced idleness cut into the family's earnings. Wolfgang suffered two bouts of rheumatic fever, at six and again at ten; these may have been the start of the chain of illness that was to kill him at thirty-five. He and Nannerl both came down with a serious attack of typhoid fever at The Hague – he was then nine; his sister nearly died and he was left skin and bone. When he was eleven they both came through smallpox in Moravia, where the family had gone to escape an epidemic. There were also the usual colds and skin troubles. 'Our professors of physic', the British Minister at The Hague reported – in a private letter written before the typhoid attack – 'don't think he will be long lived.'

More insidious were the moral and psychological effects of living perpetually on show. Wolfgang and Nannerl often played duets, but at nine he could sustain a concert on his own as player-composer (she was ill), and at all times his abilities were the prime attraction. For six weeks before their last London concert – they played from twelve to three at the Swan and Hoop in Cornhill, admittance at the cut rate of half a crown – visitors could hear them play in private, test them with unknown pieces to read at sight or improvise on, and buy concert tickets as well as engraved portraits and some of Wolfgang's first published sonatas. Leopold, an early master of public relations, drummed up custom further along the tour by sending out newspaper reports of the children's success; advertisements often understated Wolfgang's age, though by a prudent year or eighteen months. This was exploitation in the literal sense: the purpose of the first Italian tour – Leopold wrote openly to a friend – was to make the most of Wolfgang's talents before he attained 'the age and physical appearance that [would] no longer attract admiration' for them.

At the same time Leopold took great care of the children's health and well-being. Hasse thought he spoilt the boy. Wolfgang, 'soaked in

5   Maria Anna Mozart: oil painting by Rosa Hagenauer-Barducci, c. 1775. All known portraits of Mozart's mother suggest a bland, homely character.

music' as he was to describe himself in later life, could probably not have been kept from playing for much of the day whatever the circumstances. In childhood there was time for another kind of play. 'As long as the piece of music lasted', Nannerl recalled after his death, 'he was all music himself; as soon as it was over, one saw the child again' – one who, like other gifted children, had invented an imaginary kingdom (named Zurück – 'Back') and mapped it out. In London Charles Burney saw him go straight from making musical fireworks to playing at marbles, 'in the true childish way of one who knows nothing', while another observer recorded that he broke off playing the harpsichord when a favourite cat walked in, 'nor could we bring him back for a considerable time'.

Some said he wept easily and was highly susceptible; true, the eighteenth century was the age of sensibility and tears. At a difficult moment in later life Mozart wrote with some pathos that through his wandering childhood he had got used to 'leav[ing] people, countries, and cities, and with no great hope of soon, or ever again, seeing the kind friends I had left behind'. As a fourteen-year-old in Naples he had written 'I simply love travelling'; he seems to have enjoyed later travels too.

The most insidious leftover from the years of travel and adulation was his taste for luxury. When he felt (at twenty-six) that he must have that red coat with the mother-of-pearl buttons he wrote: 'I should like all my things to be of good quality, genuine and beautiful. Why is it, I wonder, that those who cannot afford it, would like to spend a fortune on such articles, and those who can, do not do so?' This goes some way to explain his later money troubles.

Yet the legacy from the early years was in many ways positive. At an age when most musicians were still feeling their way from a base of narrow experience he had not only met important people but had heard a great deal of new music and seen a great deal of theatre in all the leading European countries; he had observed characters and scenes high and low, from public hangings to royal levees; he had met some of the leading composers, performers, and musicologists. It was an incomparable training for a life of making music, opera in particular.

In London the fashionable composer Johann Christian Bach let the tiny boy play the harpsichord while standing between his legs; Wolfgang heard the great castrato Giovanni Manzuoli, who was later

6   Marianne (Nannerl) Mozart as a young girl: oil painting by Pietro Antonio Lorenzoni

to sing for him and appear in his pastoral *Ascanio in Alba*. At Florence he made fast friends (over half a week) with Thomas Linley, like him fourteen years old, a promising English composer and violinist who was to die even younger, at twenty-two. At Bologna the famous historian of music Padre G. B. Martini nudged Wolfgang through the examination that made him, at fourteen, a member of the equally famous Philharmonic Academy. A further honour in Rome made him a knight (of the papal Order of the Golden Spur). The elder, shrewder composer Gluck had this decoration and was known everywhere as the Chevalier, but Mozart dropped it after wearing it once: a young patrician joked about it, and he perhaps lacked the inches and gravitas to bring it off.

The music he wrote in these years, down to *Mitridate*, was not then taken to be his chief claim to fame; it is now seldom heard, and would scarcely be heard at all if it were by someone else. That is not to say that it is mediocre – only that many composers of the 1760s turned out agreeable pieces in an international 'galant' style, at times much alike. Many of Wolfgang's early works, written for himself to play at the keyboard, reflect J. C. Bach's Italianate version of this style, melodious, full of gentle feeling, apparently easy yet built on what Leopold called 'the thread' of sound construction. There is as yet little sense of development through conflict: the early symphony in E♭ (K 16) – these London symphonies are really three-movement overtures – has a touch of poignant feeling in the slow movement, but cannot then do much more than repeat it.

Already Wolfgang composed in most of the genres he was to master later on. When he turned out orchestrally accompanied masses and other church music he showed competence in the 'learned', contrapuntal style required in at least parts of such works. His attempt at Italian comic opera, *La finta semplice*, came of an offhand recommendation by Joseph II while the Mozarts were in Vienna in 1768; the austere Joseph took care not to be financially responsible for the opera house, and the impresario who was would not in the end put on the work. Leopold talked of 'plots' and 'persecution'; it may be that the Italian musicians in Vienna, a clannish lot, elbowed out of the way a work by a twelve-year-old outsider, but *La finta semplice* was not remarkable enough to demand a hearing. In its limpidity *Bastien und Bastienne*, a tiny Singspiel or German comic opera with spoken dialogue, held more promise.

Mitridate was Mozart's first attempt at serious opera, a highly conventional form that was already being questioned and adapted. The form sprang ultimately from the French classical tragedies of Corneille and Racine. Dialogue in recitative made way at intervals for arias that set an 'affect' or emotion while the action froze, and that gave the singers an opportunity for vocal display. Throughout the eighteenth century serious opera depended on virtuoso male sopranos, castrated before their voices broke, who deepened its artificiality. Mozart was lucky in having a solidly dramatic libretto taken from Racine himself – which is one reason why *Mitridate* still works in the theatre as his next Milan opera, *Lucio Silla* (1772), does not (even though it includes one number unmatched in the earlier work, a tomb scene for the pair of lovers and chorus that easily compasses the solemn, the terrible, and the serene, with accompanied recitative where Donna Elvira already stirs in the sighing woodwind). Both operas show Mozart unable as yet to get away from a monotonous row of full-out numbers, and making up for it, in *Lucio Silla* especially, with a profusion of instrumental music; yet the vitality of the finest arias in *Mitridate* still takes the audience by surprise.

Adolescence meant an inevitable comedown from the status of child prodigy. For Mozart it was always likely to be a difficult time. His was prolonged. His body matured slowly: he started being shaved when he was nearly twenty-two (till then his mother had cut the down on his cheeks with scissors). His psyche likewise took time to develop: he was twenty-four when for the first time he wrote his favourite 'little cousin' ('Bäsle') Maria Thekla Mozart a letter that was not a cascade of nonsense language ferrying obscenities and innuendoes, most of them cloacal.

From the 'Bäsle' letters springs the *Amadeus* myth of Mozart as sublime lout; they have also persuaded some biographers that Wolfgang and Maria Thekla were lovers, perhaps in a physical sense. This seems unlikely.

Mozart's sexual life outside marriage is almost certainly unknowable. He was highly susceptible to women; his feelings for them as for much else came out in play: play with words and jokes and domestic romps around the furniture, Cherubino chasing Susanna. From puberty he seems to have been in love with one Salzburg girl after another; when away from the town he teased Nannerl about them in at times ciphered postscripts to his family letters.

He first met Maria Thekla, his uncle Franz Alois's daughter, when he was seven and once more at the age of ten; she was two years younger. What set off the notorious letters was his visit to Augsburg in 1777, when he was twenty-one. She was, he told his father, 'beautiful, intelligent, clever, and gay . . . we two get on extremely well, for, like myself, she is a bit of a scamp'. The following was the kind of thing he wrote to the 'Bäsle' herself from his next stop:

> Forgive my wretched writing, but the pen is already worn to a shred, and I've been shitting, so 'tis said, nigh twenty-two years through the same old hole, which is not yet frayed one whit, though I've used it daily to shit, and each time the muck with my teeth I've bit . . . [the next sentence in French:] I kiss your hands, your face, your knees, and your – well, whatever you permit me to kiss ['baiser', a verb with a double meaning].

Much more of this followed in later letters. It needs to be put in context. The lavatory jokes were, as we know, common in Mozart's family (though as a rule fewer). The rhymes, jokes, and other verbal byplay erupted all over Wolfgang's correspondence and even on his scores: he later annotated the solo part in a horn concerto, written for his friend Joseph Leutgeb, with 'Over to you, Mr Donkey . . . quick . . . come on . . . courage . . . [above a four-bar rest:] what, finished already?' The translator of his letters, Emily Anderson, wrote that in many of them, 'while expressing himself in words, [he] seems in reality to be thinking in terms of music': he would write words or sentences backwards like an inverted musical phrase (signing himself 'Gnagflow Trazom', 'The Germany from post has not yet arrived'), devise Joycean puns like dissonant chords ('Merditeranischen'), or go off into a run of variations ('You may trust, believe, opine, hold the

7 Maria Thekla Mozart, the 'Bäsle' ('little cousin') to whom Mozart addressed
jokily obscene letters. The self-portrait in pencil suggests a strong character
as well as some artistic ability.

opinion, cherish the constant hope, consider, imagine, think and be
confident that we are well, but I can assure you of the fact').

The letters to Maria Thekla have their share of nonsense rhymes ('I
am very sorry to hear that the Abbot rabbit has had another stroke so
soon moon') and verbal cataracts ('Croatians, damnations . . . Jesuits,

Augustinians, Benedictines, Capuchins' etc., line upon line); only here do we find Mozart playing with genital imagery and language; but their dominant import is cloacal ('I shit on your nose and it will run down your chin . . . Sleep soundly, my love, into your mouth your arse you'll shove'). This marks them as a well-known kind of adolescent foolery, in which an unripe, muddled sexual awareness has young people daring each other to cap a gross pleasantry with a grosser one amid fits of giggles. What makes the letters noteworthy is that they have been preserved: such bubblings-up are seldom written down. About Mozart they tell us chiefly that he took time to grow up.

To his parents and sister he always presented himself as the affectionate son and brother. (The view that by addressing Nannerl in postscripts to the letters he sent his father he was purposely denying her an individual hearing is an anachronism: at a time when postage was dear and letters were passed round the family it was common form). Little is known of how they all got on from late 1773 to mid-1777, when they were in Salzburg almost throughout: these are among the least documented years in Mozart's life. The crisis in his relationship with his father came in 1777–78, when he went on tour to south Germany and Paris accompanied only by his mother.

The tour was to be a disaster. Mozart failed to land a job, failed to make money, failed to compose as much as he needed to, fell in love with a young woman singer his parents disapproved of, and halfway through the tour, in Paris, his mother died.

Leopold would have gone with them if he had been able. As it was he could scarcely bear not to be on hand and in control: 'Wherever you stay, you will always, will you not, get the servant to put boot-trees into your boots?' He stayed behind because a new prince-archbishop forced him to. The old archbishop had made Leopold deputy Kapellmeister (court composer) in 1763 and Wolfgang concertmaster (a minor post) in 1769, had allowed them extended leaves to go on tour, and had subsidised the tours themselves either by keeping on Leopold's salary or by making an outright grant. He died, however, and was succeeded in 1772 by another nobleman, Hieronymus

Colloredo. The new prince-archbishop was awkward, in particular about granting the Mozarts leave. In 1777 he theoretically discharged both father and son, but in practice Leopold had to stay on to keep earning his salary. This was by then a necessity: we do not know how much the earlier tours with the two miraculous children had earned, but expenses on the road and in such places as London and Paris were high; it does not seem that much if anything was left. Leopold, by his own account, had to go into debt to finance his son's latest tour.

The purpose of the tour was to secure for Wolfgang a job away from Salzburg. Father and son were by then thoroughly dissatisfied with conditions in the archbishopric. They could not both get away, but Wolfgang at least might find a better post with one of the German courts. Other possibilities they considered as the tour went on were a trip to Paris (where some German musicians were well established and concerts might pay) or a commission to write one more opera in Italy, perhaps for the royal theatre at Naples: 'I have an inexpressible longing to write another opera', Wolfgang declared when a chance seemed to offer. Leopold did not rule this out, but he insisted that a permanent post, most likely in Germany, was an essential base; Wolfgang, like others, might then get leave for a season in Italy.

Their correspondence is one of the most pathetic and intriguing records ever kept of dealings between father and son. We need to bear in mind that an eighteenth-century bachelor of twenty-two was not an autonomous being. Until he married or was otherwise 'emancipated' by his father he was expected to obey his parents and help to support them. The family mattered more than the individual. The current social code underwrote Leopold in expecting his son to '[make] your father's happiness your first consideration'; nor did Wolfgang openly question it. When Leopold, in a crisis, reminded him that as a child he had prized his father's ability to plan and foresee and had often said 'Next to God comes Papa', Wolfgang replied 'I still cling to [the motto]'; in congratulating Leopold on his name day he professed 'eternal obedience'; as another St Leopold's day approached he prayed (though it might sound 'strange and perhaps ridiculous') to be able to congratulate his father on it throughout his own life – a suggestion here that he might prefer not to shed his childhood skin. He made out – not always truthfully – that he was obeying his father's directions, and in practice he did so, though late and browbeaten.

Leopold, then, had custom and morality on his side; he was worldly wise and showed that, on a perhaps superficial level, he knew how his son's mind worked. (He guessed, for instance, that Wolfgang in a tight corner had pawned his dead mother's watch.) Even in contemporary terms, all the same, he was a heavy father. He tried to control his son in all his doings, not just the use of boot-trees but wine-drinking and sacramental confession; Wolfgang had to reassure him that he was moderate in the first and regular in the second. Above all, he sought to control Wolfgang's management of his budding career – and this by slow post.

As he did so Leopold showed an unpleasing streak of self-pity. He expressed it in terms of the sentimental drama of the period. If Wolfgang drank too much, 'picture to yourself in what unhappiness and distress you would plunge your dear mother in a far distant country, not to mention myself'. The crisis over Wolfgang's proposing to follow his young singer and her family brought him out in complaints that he was in debt, Nannerl had sacrificed her savings to guarantee a further loan, his clothes were shabby and he could not afford new ones. Worse was to follow.

Leopold's basic complaint about his son is best summed up in words he used a few years later, in 1782, when he was calmer: Wolfgang's 'outstanding fault', he wrote to a noblewoman who had befriended his son, was

> that he is far too *patient*, or rather *easygoing*, too indolent, perhaps even too proud, in short, that he is the sum total of all those traits which render a man *inactive*; on the other hand, he is too *impatient*, too *hasty*, and will not bide his time. Two opposing elements rule his nature, I mean, there is either too much or too little, never the golden mean. If he is not actually in want, then he is immediately satisfied and

becomes indolent and lazy. If he has to bestir himself, then he realises his worth and wants to make his fortune at once.

There is evidence that in worldly terms Leopold was right. Wolfgang had his own justification, but it was not of a kind at once to secure an income.

He began his tour in late September 1777 at Munich, where the Elector of Bavaria at first let him know that he ought to make a name in Italy, then, still without having heard Mozart play, said directly that there was no job going. Mozart annoyed his father by entertaining a proposal that he should be subsidised by ten local men in exchange for new compositions; he had had such a deal from a great nobleman (who had at once died), but to multiply it by ten and make it stick was unlikely to say the least. At Augsburg he had trouble securing a concert and even then was out of pocket. So at least he wrote home, but as we know he misled his father about other things (such as the number of new works he had composed) a question hovers over his rather frequent statements, on this and later tours, that his concerts had lost money or had made very little: was he concealing losses of another kind? He then went on to Mannheim, the seat of the Elector Palatine; there, from late October, he stayed.

The Elector, Karl Theodor, to begin with seemed to show favour: he heard Mozart play, paid him (though only with a gold watch), let him teach his illegitimate children, and said, in the careless way of great persons, that a German opera 'could easily be arranged'. He kept Mozart hanging on until 8 December, when he too said there was no job going. There was no opera either. On 31 December news came of the death of the Elector of Bavaria; this made Karl Theodor ruler of Bavaria, plunged the court into mourning, and stopped public performances. Yet Mozart stayed on until 14 March 1778, with a short excursion in January to the country house of Princess Caroline of Nassau-Weilburg, a member of the Dutch ruling family for whom he had played as a child.

He had – just – the means to enable him to stay: he gave lessons to two pupils and engaged to write some flute concertos and flute quartets for an amateur, a commission he seems to have misrepresented to Leopold, and typically left unfinished. He had two strong reasons for staying. One was the famous Mannheim orchestra: at a time when orchestral music was by no means the preferred form, it was unique in its attack and especially its control of volume. Mozart got to know some of its musicians, in particular the music director, Christian Cannabich; he gave piano lessons to Cannabich's daughter Rosa and, he said, portrayed her in the slow movement of the piano sonata in C (K. 309); he was probably in love with her for a time. His excitement at discovering the town's musical resources can be felt in the sinfonia concertante in E♭ for violin and viola (K. 364): though written in Salzburg after his return, it embodies the symphonic potential and mighty crescendo of the Mannheim orchestra as well as the 'singing' abilities of its solo players. He had found a new musical world.

The other reason was his meeting, at an unknown date but perhaps as early as November, the family of a music copyist called Fridolin Weber. This man had four daughters, three of them budding singers; Mozart fell in love with the second daughter, Aloisia, then about sixteen, a soprano able to do justice to a difficult aria in *Lucio Silla*. Only on 17 January 1778 did Mozart mention the Webers to his father; he then went off with them to appear at Princess Caroline's – for very little money.

Until then he and his father had agreed, after Leopold had begun to doubt the chances of a post in Germany, that he should go to Paris in the company of two German musicians and there run a well-prepared campaign of concert-giving; his mother would return to Salzburg. On getting back to Mannheim from Princess Caroline's, however, Wolfgang wrote on 4 February that he no longer wished to go to Paris: instead he proposed to go off with the Webers. 'I have become so fond of this unfortunate family that my dearest wish is to make them happy' (or, as Frau Mozart commented in a secret postscript, 'when Wolfgang makes new acquaintances, he immediately wants to give his life and property for them'). They might go to Italy, where he would write a serious opera for Aloisia to appear in; 'I think we shall go to Switzerland

and perhaps also to Holland.' Fridolin struck him as just like his father; when he was with the Webers 'I found my torn clothes mended.'

This letter, Leopold wrote, 'almost killed me'. By then he and his son had had a long passage of arms. Leopold was irritated almost from the start of the tour by Wolfgang's 'careless' response to his repeated, minute directions. He apologised once or twice for having been 'peevish', but still insisted on being right about trifles, such as the date of a letter. He guessed, correctly, that his son was losing or at any rate not making money, and that he was failing to take the obvious road to success: he should court the right people, not waste time or make himself cheap, and, if he did get to write a German opera, should choose 'the natural and popular style, which everyone understands'. The grand Mannheim style – which he knew his son was interested in – must be left for grand subjects: 'everything in its place'. If Wolfgang went to Paris 'there must be attention and daily concentration on earning some money, and you must cultivate extreme politeness in order to ingratiate yourself with people of standing'. It was no joke, he added, to have to live on whatever you could make on tour – and it was not reassuring then to get from Wolfgang a letter, half of it nonsense greetings to the whole alphabet: 'Papa be annoyed not must. I that just like today feel.'

To reproaches about his 'carelessness' Wolfgang replied:

if you attribute it to my negligence, thoughtlessness, and laziness, I can only thank you for your good opinion of me and sincerely regret that you do not know your own son. I am not careless, I am simply prepared for anything and am able, in consequence, to wait patiently for whatever may come, and endure it – provided that my honour and the good name of Mozart are not affected . . . come what may, all is well, so long as a man enjoys good health. For happiness consists – simply in imagination.

Four days later he wrote, as the Elector still dawdled: 'I have resigned myself entirely to the will of God.' Leopold countered that God's will did not excuse one from planning one's future; imagination did not make for happiness if you were stranded without money.

There was here, and there would continue to be, a generational clash. Leopold was the heedful craftsman in an age when such a figure depended on a patron, Wolfgang the prototype modern artist confident of his own genius. (He soon declared grandly that he would stop giving lessons – something his father was having to do to make ends meet – because 'I am a composer and was born to be a Kapellmeister. I neither can nor ought to bury the talent for composition with which God in his goodness has so richly endowed me . . .') A useful sidelight comes from the autobiography of an early twentieth-century painter, Gino Severini, who was the son of a low-paid courtroom usher. In Paris Severini was several times evicted for non-payment of rent, he might have no idea where his next meal was coming from, but, he points out, whereas a courtroom usher knows that he will always be poor an artist has other resources: a painting that really works, even a sale, may turn up at any time. He therefore stuck to his art at the cost of ill health. Mozart was an early example of this self-belief – in him, totally justified. True, in 1777–78 it rather spoilt the effect that he stayed dependent on his father both for money and, in the end, for marching orders.

The letter about the Webers that 'almost killed' Leopold brought him crashing down in massive reproof. He went over all his son's earlier failings in detail, presumed love affairs included (with Maria Thekla among others). Wolfgang's latest notion of going off with the Webers to all points of the compass was 'whimsical . . . ill-considered . . . impractical'. He did not, then or later, rule out a professional or even, by implication, a passing sexual tie between his son and Aloisia Weber, but he spelt out in detail the awful results of sacrificing the interests of the Mozarts to those of the Webers:

> now it depends solely on your good sense and your way of life
> whether you die as an ordinary musician, utterly forgotten by the
> world, or as a famous kapellmeister, of whom posterity will read, –
> whether, captured by some woman, you die bedded on straw in an
> attic full of starving children, or whether, after a Christian life spent
> in contentment, honour, and renown, you leave this world with your
> family well provided for and your name respected by all.

Such melodrama was realistic enough – poor musicians did die on straw, children did starve – but it did not touch Wolfgang inwardly. The need to assert his independence was strong even though he could do little to put it into practice. In the same formidable letter, his father appealed pathetically to their old bedtime games; he replied: 'Those days when, standing on a chair, I used to sing to you *Oragna fiagata fa* and finish by kissing you on the tip of your nose are gone indeed; but do I honour, love and obey you any the less on that account? I will say no more.'

Nevertheless Leopold had ordered him peremptorily '*Off with you to Paris!* and that soon! Find your place among great people. *Aut Caesar aut nihil* [either Caesar or nothing].' Frau Mozart would go to Paris with him, obviously to keep him in order.

Wolfgang gave way. He had – he said – written on impulse and had not really meant to go off at once with the Webers. He was 'clean-minded' and had no 'evil designs' on Aloisia or, for that matter, on Maria Thekla. He apologised for sometimes getting 'excited' – 'if that is the expression I should use, though indeed I would much rather say, if I sometimes write naturally'. As Leopold kept up a drizzle of reproaches he wrote 'I have full confidence in three friends, all of them powerful and invincible, God, your head, and mine'; where his head did not as yet equal his father's he hoped it would catch up. But he went, without question, to Paris.

There he failed. His failure was professional and social; the two went hand in hand. He was able almost at once to write a symphony for the Concert Spirituel, the main concert series, but could not then have a sinfonia concertante (K. 297b) performed. He composed a large part of a ballet but got no credit for it. He found three pupils; for one of them and her father, a duke, he wrote a flute and harp concerto, but the duke, as he reported, failed to pay for that or for the lessons (Mozart had failed to ask at the right moment) and went out of town. He announced a French opera, an important undertaking, though he also expressed scorn for French music and singing and the opera seems never to have got off the ground. There was talk of his being appointed court organist at Versailles, but he would have none of it: he must be court composer or nothing. His dealings with the high aristocracy irked him: they kept him waiting in a cold room, then gave him neither attention nor money. It all made him want to go to Italy.

Then, on 3 July 1778, his mother died. Her illness is obscure and was short; she insisted on a German doctor and Mozart, by his own account, showed little competence in finding one; the doctor came four days late. Wolfgang wrote his father a letter to prepare him for the news, as often before upholding the will of God. He did not say so, but his behaviour points to deep grief and, later, depression.

He moved in with an old patron of the family, Baron Melchior Grimm, a German but a member of the 'enlightened' group of French intellectuals. Grimm wished to help; he had views on opera and may have persuaded Mozart to value fast-moving action and subordinate the libretto to the music. In Parisian aesthetic disputes Grimm was, however, opposed to traditional French opera, while Mozart wished to master it as Gluck had. He was also something of a dry stick. He presently told Leopold that Mozart did not get about enough, and could have done with 'half the talent and twice the social skills'. In Paris you needed to be 'tough, enterprising, bold'; Mozart was none of these.

Grimm's letter confirmed Leopold in everything he had – as usual rightly – suspected. From the start he had urged his son to court the great, to conform to French taste, in effect to take the money and run, to Italy if he wished. He now urged him to publish 'something short, easy, and popular' in J. C. Bach's style: 'what is slight can still be great'. Mozart, however, had left J. C. Bach and short, easy pieces behind; he was neither willing to court the great nor good at it; in Paris musical politics, which called for smoothness, persistence, and repartee, he was a non-starter. Paris, he wrote a fortnight after his mother's death, was 'totally opposed to my genius, inclinations, knowledge, and sympathies'.

Leopold had all along kept up his usual complaints and bursts of self-pity. By late August 1778 he had grasped Mozart's failure in Paris.

He now decided that his son should go back to the old Salzburg job of concertmaster – which he had managed to have reinstated – with Munich and Italy held out as later possibilities. At the same time he disclosed to Wolfgang his mother's secret postscript from Mannheim, about her son's readiness to sacrifice everything for the Webers. He added: 'If your mother had returned home from Mannheim' – as she would have but for the Weber affair – 'she would not have died.' Though the next sentence stated that Divine Providence had in any case fixed the date of Frau Mozart's death, this was to rub in the son's sense of guilt for his mother's death. It was unforgivable; we may question whether Wolfgang forgave it, then or later.

Mozart agreed to go back to Salzburg, though he put up a smokescreen: he made a show of laying down conditions, and claimed that his affairs in Paris were now 'beginning to prosper'; if he could hold out there 'for a few years', 'I should certainly get on very well'. Grimm – with whom he now quarrelled – in effect bundled him out of Paris on 26 September. He spent a month in Nancy and Strasbourg, giving concerts which (he once again reported) paid very little. Against Leopold's wishes, he went on to Mannheim. The Webers were no longer there – they had followed the Elector to Munich, where Aloisia now had a contract to sing in opera – but a new musical find took hold of Mozart, the 'monodrama' or 'melodrama', a spoken play with orchestral accompaniment: he agreed to write one, unpaid. He also talked of after all getting an appointment in Mannheim, where he fancied the Elector (and the Webers) would soon return.

Leopold was by then furious. 'I shall go mad or die of a decline.' His son was driving him further into debt while building 'castles in the air': on 19 November he told Wolfgang to come home as soon as possible. Wolfgang did not answer (he hinted that he could not bear to), but he still dawdled through south Germany on his way to Munich. He got there on Christmas Day only to find that Aloisia was no longer interested in him.

Leopold, totally exasperated at this further delay, wrote on 28 December: 'I command you to leave at once, for your conduct is disgraceful . . . or am I to take the mail coach myself and fetch you?' Mozart gave two explanations: he needed to present some sonatas to the Electress (and wait for the reward); he was held back by fear that he had lost his father's love. On the latter point he had been reassured by a Salzburg friend, and saw no cause to dread his father's reproaches: 'I am guilty of no fault (by fault I mean something which does not become a Christian and a man of honour).' He none the less hung on for the first performance of an opera, and at length reached Salzburg about the middle of January 1779.

What happened to Mozart in the six and a half months that ran from his mother's death to his homecoming we can only guess. His letters hide as much as they reveal. The chances are that he was in a turmoil of grief and some guilt about his mother, and of anger at his father, at Grimm, at the Parisians, at the adult world in general. Unusually long periods when he did not write home suggest as much; they also raise the question of what he was up to when, for instance, he stuck for a month in Nancy and Strasbourg. The musicologist Alfred Einstein was sure the piano sonata in A minor (K. 310), written in Paris after Frau Mozart's death, was 'most personal', with no trace of the 'sociability' then expected. The big first movement wanders in its development section through blasted heaths of feeling, the Andante sounds drained, the Presto tense and anguished. True, we tend to think stormy, tragic utterance must be personal, and calm, cheerful music impersonal – a Romantic illusion. The fact remains that Mozart – as he half confessed to his father – wrote very little at the time other than this sonata.

Being jilted by Aloisia was a further blow. 'I can only weep', he wrote to Leopold in what he felt to be an unusually intimate confession. This, as it happened, crossed Leopold's 'I command you' letter of 27 December. Mozart was embittered, showed it, but remained 'until death your most obedient son'. Leopold on his side tried to pick up some of the pieces. In late November he was still writing that his son was 'just thoughtless' – 'You will be all right in time!' This note vanished as he grew more exasperated, though he too remained 'your loving father'.

In answering the 'I command you' letter Wolfgang picked up his father's reference to the 'gay dreams' that had distracted him. They were, he said, scarcely gay. 'Peaceful dreams, refreshing, sweet dreams! That is what they are – dreams which, if realised, would make my life, which is more sad than cheerful, more endurable.' Here again was the divide between generations. Leopold's was realistic, obedient to a God who was himself maker and keeper of a rational universe, not deeply touched by the sentiment poured forth in the works of Sterne, Rousseau, or the young Goethe. Wolfgang heralded the coming of those for whom dream would be ultimate reality.

He and his father and sister then lived together in Salzburg through nearly the whole of 1779–80. About these two years, Mozart's compositions and performances apart, we know almost nothing. Wolfgang and Leopold were soon embattled, now on the same side and against another man in authority they took to be oppressive, their employer the prince-archbishop. Wolfgang would free himself from oppression with the sword of art – his triumph in creating, in the winter of 1780–81, the opera he had failed to write in Paris, *Idomeneo*. This it was that gave him the confidence to leave the archbishop's service and set himself up in Vienna as an independent musician. When he took that step he also, we may hazard, made good – as far as anyone can in this life – his escape from the father.

2 The conflict with authority

Count Hieronymus Colloredo, last prince-archbishop of Salzburg, is remembered because he and Mozart quarrelled and his chamberlain threw out the young composer with the notorious kick in the pants. He has often been called a fool or a bully. Yet he was a reformer; from his own point of view he had good reason to thwart the Mozarts.

At his accession in 1772 Colloredo was forty, already a prince of the Church as well as a nobleman with high-ranking connections in Vienna. He agreed with Joseph II's 'enlightened' policy and set out to apply it in Salzburg. He imposed austerity on an ample church life: his purpose was both to save time and money and to establish a 'purer' form of worship. Sung masses were not to last more than three-quarters of an hour; intelligible words must take precedence; by 1780–82 German hymns were on and instrumental music (organ excepted) was off. Court music too, which had run on for half the night, was now held to little over an hour. These dictates were not always literally carried out, even at the cathedral, unless Colloredo was officiating. Musicians had none the less been warned: like other subordinates, they must be economical, sober, and diligent.

'Enlightened' policy of this sort had nothing to do with conferring freedom. The new prince-archbishop, like Joseph II, was an autocrat. Nor did it mean promoting native musicians. Colloredo, again like Joseph – and like his own predecessor – was musically literate; all three assumed the best musicians were Italian – a common view when

Italian opera dominated musical Europe (but for France). Leopold Mozart twice saw a middling Italian appointed as court composer in preference to himself; he remained deputy to the end of his life, from 1763 to 1787.

Not that Leopold had clearly earned the top post. He had taken years of leave to display his children around Europe, and had more than once got additional time off on a pretext – as when he hoped to secure for Wolfgang a post with the Habsburg ruler of Tuscany, Joseph II's brother; he did it again soon after Colloredo's accession. To a ruling prince, servants – such as the Mozarts – ought to attend faithfully, behave deferentially, and do the job they were paid for. In a hierarchical society, a musician who left a court post to perform in this town and that could appear to 'go about begging'. Colloredo used the expression about the Mozarts' tours – just as Maria Theresia, some years earlier, had discouraged another of her sons from giving Wolfgang a post in Milan: why burden himself with 'useless' people 'of that sort'? 'If they are in your service it degrades that service when these people go about the world like beggars.' (It had been amusing to let the six-year-old Wolfgang kiss her and play for her; it was another matter to take on a wandering musician, nearly grown up.)

Many composers fell in with these expectations, notably Haydn, who wore Prince Esterhazy's livery until the year before Mozart's death. Leopold, however, chafed at them. He sneered at the archbishop and his officials and led his son to do so. In a small town and court their hostility would have been known even if – at a time when governments steamed letters open – the cipher they sometimes resorted to in their correspondence had been harder to break.

Wolfgang, appointed third concertmaster in 1769, was to begin with unpaid – a kind of apprenticeship, implying that he would be paid later on, as he was from 1772. The salary, 150 florins a year – less than one-third of his father's – was modest; the contemporary British equivalent, about £16, was only a farm labourer's wage, but the exchange rate made Britain notoriously expensive for continentals. In

Salzburg that amount stretched a good deal further; Wolfgang was in any case living with his parents.

The duties of the post included composing both secular and church music and helping with rehearsals. after his failed tour of 1777–79 to south Germany and Paris Wolfgang was made court organist, a post previously held by an honoured friend of his family, Cajetan Adlgasser, who had died; the salary was 450 florins, 50 florins less than his father's. The tour thus marked a break in Mozart's Salzburg career. It raised his salary, but to nothing like what he deserved; it left him still more alienated from Salzburg, more eager to get away, yet burdened with the evidence the tour had supplied that he was unlikely to win a better post elsewhere.

What was expected of him in his new post is clear from the barbed remarks in a later document appointing Michael Haydn (Joseph Haydn's younger brother, a long-standing Salzburg musician): Michael's duties were to be the same as 'young Mozart's', 'with the additional stipulation that he show more diligence, instruct the chapel [choir] boys [in keyboard playing], and compose more often for our cathedral and church music'.

Mozart may have stinted the choirboys' lessons, but the dig at his alleged idleness as composer was unfair. In his Salzburg years he wrote 'music for use', steadily and in abundance.

The town afforded greater opportunities than one might think from Mozart's dismissive remarks, made in 1778–79 when he was already at odds with Colloredo and under stress from his failure in Paris. Salzburg, he then wrote, 'is no place for my talent'; its orchestra had no clarinets, its chapel no great singers; its musicians lacked the seriousness and discipline of those he had found at Mannheim; they were 'coarse, slovenly, dissolute', always off to the pub; Salzburgers' language and manners were 'quite intolerable to me'.

These diatribes held a touch of special pleading. The town offered a monarchical court, several great churches, a university, a local aristocracy, substantial merchants, all of them patrons who frequently commissioned music. Two countesses were among Wolfgang's patrons, two future medical men of his own age among his closest friends. A generation earlier, such conditions had been enough – some grumbling apart – for J. S. Bach.

Mozart, however, was the new type of musician who saw himself as an individual artist; furthermore, he knew he was the best. He was right, though injudicious in showing it: near the start of the 1777–79 tour, when he hoped the Elector of Bavaria might give him a job, he offered to take on all the composers in Munich and a few from Italy, France, Germany, England, and Spain. His genius, besides, was more dramatic than contemplative. To such a composer the new limits on Salzburg church music must be damaging: Wolfgang turned out plenty of masses (five in 1775–76 alone) but some were routine works. Above all, he longed to compose Italian opera, the form most coveted by an ambitious eighteenth-century musician. Salzburg, however, did not afford it except once in a long while; even serious plays (which often required music) turned up only now and then.

Already during the early Salzburg years Mozart was bound to feel frustrated by the lack of opportunities in the theatre. He managed to write an Italian comic opera, *La finta giardiniera* (1775), but that was for Munich; it made little headway. Salzburg, in the old prince-archbishop's time, had put on *La finta semplice*, the work by the child prodigy that Vienna had ignored. But for his descents on Italy, however (the last in 1772), Mozart had no chance to write anything more dramatic than a pastoral, a flattering allegory, or the choruses for a solemn play. Only after the Paris tour, in 1780, did Munich at last offer a great opportunity. Not by chance, it turned out also to be his way out of Salzburg and princely service.

Meanwhile the works he wrote for the court and the town signalled a new artistic maturity. From the mid-1770s, they embody the classical style, first defined by Mozart and Haydn. This subsumed the near-exhausted 'galant' and 'learned' forms of Western music in a new synthesis that overcame both. Its identifying mark, Charles Rosen has written, is 'the symmetrical resolution of opposing forces': firm control of tonality makes for symmetry, subtle control of harmonic tension and varied rhythm along the way create the dramatically opposed forces to be reconciled. This 'style of reinterpretation' gives a phrase a wholly new significance by putting it in another context, above all by modulation. Rosen's masterly study needs to be read as a whole; anyone who has become aware of the light and shade Mozart could work through unlooked-for modulation, the dramatic knots untied by the end of a piece, will profit from his close analysis. But even to an untrained ear Mozart's Salzburg works from 1773 on are clearly 'Mozartian'.

In these years he wrote a great deal. Mozart as a spontaneous artist who composed music in his head and wrote it down without a second thought is a romantic fiction. He did say at one time 'composing is my sole delight and passion', at another, 'everything has been composed, but not yet written down'. If time pressed he could write fast: in 1783 he was to write the 'Linz' symphony in C (K. 425) in five days. Arriving at a version that satisfied him, though, often called for hard work with pen and keyboard. Of his many unfinished sketches some were abandoned because they seemed to him not to work. At the same time he was willing to turn out the musical equivalent of journalism – craftsmanlike pieces done to order that did not engage him deeply.

These last form the background to his Salzburg period, especially in 1772–77, before the tour to Paris. There was a demand for entertainment music during some feast or other jollification or to frame a concert – pieces for combinations of string or wind instruments called 'divertimento', 'cassation', 'serenade', or indeed string quartets or symphonies, for in the early Salzburg years these forms did not imply the seriousness of purpose they later attained, thanks in large part to Mozart himself and to Haydn. Symphonies were just shifting from the Italian three-movement overture to the Viennese four-movement type, with minuet and trio. Serenades for winds alone were music to be performed, as a rule, in the open on summer nights, vying for attention with breezes, social chat, a torch, a passing face.

High-stepping good humour prevails in 1772 works like the symphonies in E♭ and D (K. 132–3), and the two divertimenti in D – serenades, rather (K. 131 and 136). So does a willingness to experiment with folk-like tunes (the charming flute-and-strings dialogue in the Andante of K. 133) or Haydnish deliberate argument as in the Andante of K. 132; Alfred Einstein heard its fragmented structure as rebellious 'expressionism', but we might call it jerky. By 1774 Mozart was capable of writing a symphony in the fully worked out classical style, the well-known one in A (K. 201), and another we might call grim, that in G minor (K. 183). By 1776–79, on either side of his Paris venture, he was composing divertimenti for string quartet and two horns (K. 247, 287, 334) that Einstein called 'among the purest, gayest, most satisfying, and most perfect' compositions ever, 'a lost paradise of music'.

A stern elegance informs the Allegro moderato first movement of the A major symphony, right from the soft *piano* start in the midst of the opening theme – which then passes round the orchestra, growing the while more intense and more diverse. The Andante (muted strings and dotted rhythms) is serene and spare, the minuet rumbustious, the final movement a true Allegro con spirito, dramatically developed. In each movement a graceful or restful second theme sets off the urgency of the first. The rushing scale passages for strings that punctuate the last movement and bring it to a laconic end are only one of the devices that make the work classical. Its note is economical, expressive force delicately balanced; no more need be said.

The 'little' G minor symphony with its relentless thrust, made the more urgent in the opening Allegro con brio by repeated syncopated notes (eerie, too, at quieter moments), has led some to think of a personal crisis; its thrusting quality runs through all movements save the Andante – even here the growling bassoon appoggiaturas give utterance to a 'rising sequence of sighs', in Stanley Sadie's words – and the trio for winds, a breath of Austrian fresh air. Other composers, notably Haydn, were then writing minor-mode symphonies of like urgency, some of which Mozart knew; these have been seen as part of the 'storm and stress' movement in Germany, a herald of Romanticism. Neal Zaslaw, on the other hand, objects that the literary movement came later: these musical bursts of tension must have their origin in satiety with the 'galant' style and a return to the earlier baroque.

A wider explanation is needed. The impulse to deep pathos had already come from Richardson's *Clarissa* and Rousseau's *La Nouvelle Héloïse*, both read by the educated all over Europe; so, from Richardson and others, had an interest in unconscious, at times dark human motivation. In all the arts the more aware practitioners felt, from the 1760s, a need for starker, purer forms and deeper feeling. Mozart shared in this concern. Not only the 'little' G minor but the striking choruses and orchestral interludes for the play *Thamos, King of Egypt* (often taken to be Masonic because the author was a Freemason, though many more could have shared in their praise of virtue and loyalty) belong to this wider proto-Romantic movement. The *Thamos* music, probably written at different times between 1773 and 1779–80, runs to stark expressiveness and some harmonies contemporaries might have called 'terrific', as they did scenes in Gothic novels that gave one an enjoyable shiver. Like the symphony, these pieces may, all the same, give utterance to an inner turmoil. For Salzburg in 1773 the 'little' G minor was scarcely entertainment music.

The mature divertimenti and other occasional music of the late Salzburg period culminated in the serenade in B♭ for thirteen instruments, all winds save for a double bass – nowadays replaced by a contrabassoon (K. 361). This, probably written in Vienna soon after Mozart's arrival in 1781, is at once extraordinarily rich and mysterious. Its seven movements, a hard task for wind players, are unflaggingly various; their shifting moods and combinations of instruments, each pair with its own tint and character, make the work an adventure of the spirit. The pulse that rules the first Adagio – made up of a rhythmic figure on the same note (of three quavers, two slurred, one accented), and an ostinato bass – runs under long waves of melody to work a kaleidoscope of harmonies and timbres. It beats for steadfastness and evanescence both, as in night-scented flowers; this is a *notturno*, a night piece. The oboes' intimations of mortality in the opening Largo are answered, five movements later, in their brief song of happiness (next-to-last of a set of masterly variations) above murmured arpeggios; their hints were earlier deepened in the weird up-and-down chord sequences of the B♭ minor trio to the second minuet. The brighter movements distil a joy at once reasonable and complex: the world is good, but it holds secrets.

Mozart's other main achievement in his native town was a series of keyboard works. The most triumphant was the piano concerto in E♭ (K. 271), written in 1777 for the touring virtuoso Mlle Jeunehomme; it was preceded by the piano sonatas K. 279–84, a set written for Munich, and followed by those written in Mannheim and Paris, K. 309–11, a harvest meagre in numbers though of high value. Together with Mozart's other works of the mid-1770s they show why he grew ever more impatient of the Salzburg yoke.

Already in 1775 he and his father saw the archbishop as hostile; Wolfgang could 'breathe freely' only away from Salzburg. In 1777, when they were planning Wolfgang's tour to south Germany and Paris, Colloredo to begin with failed to answer their petition for leave, then allowed Wolfgang's only, then took it back. Leopold drafted a further address in his most pedantic style, in which Wolfgang asked for his discharge with a reference to the parable of the talents in the Gospel: it would not do to leave his talent hidden. The archbishop scrawled 'Father and son herewith granted permission to seek their fortune according to the Gospel.' For both to lose their posts was unthinkable; Leopold managed to save his, and later secured a new one for Wolfgang at the end of the Paris tour (the archbishop seems to have been peremptory rather than vengeful).

At the final crisis in 1781 the Salzburg chamberlain, Count Karl Arco, made a grievance of Mozart's not having spent time in the prince's anteroom. Mozart did not see why he should '[idle] away a couple of hours every morning'; he had always come when sent for. Yet anteroom duty was normal for a musician in post. No wonder he had trouble getting a job in courts where his music was thought highly of: great persons scented a lack of deference. He was quick to note personal slights, as when his uncle, a respectable merchant, was kept waiting 'like a lackey' by an Augsburg grandee. 'No cringing, for I cannot bear that', he wrote when his father proposed to recommend him to another prince-bishop. He was the new man of the age, aware that his wealth, unlike a nobleman's, was in his brains – 'and those no one can take from us'. He liked to make fun of the pomp the great surrounded themselves with: when he stayed at a sovereign abbot's where the military guard called out at night 'Who goes there?' he replied 'Guess!' Mozart and court service were incompatible.

By March 1781, when Colloredo took him to Vienna with the rest of the household, he found himself seated at table below the personal valets and above the cooks – and that was just after he had achieved his grandest work so far, his Munich opera *Idomeneo*. The Elector Karl Theodor had rightly called it 'magnificent'; to Mozart it was liberating, proof of his genius. 'There is music in my opera for all kinds of people, but not for the long-eared', he had told his father ('ass' was one of his terms for the archbishop in his transparent cipher).

Once in Vienna, he longed to play it to the emperor; he was utterly frustrated when Colloredo kept him to his duties and thus stopped him from appearing at a private concert where Joseph II would be a guest. Vienna, he saw, was 'the land of the keyboard'; there he could give concerts, earn a thousand florins a year, write a German opera, help to support his father (as he now undertook to do); besides, the widowed Frau Weber now lived there with her daughters and he was perhaps already falling in love with Aloisia's sister Constanze. Was he to give up all this 'for the sake of a malevolent prince who plagues me every day and only pays me a lousy salary'?

Leopold, though he disliked the archbishop as much as his son did, urged caution. It was too late. Wolfgang grudgingly took his advice to go back to Salzburg, but as the household was about to leave town early in May he moved out to the Webers' flat. Challenged by Colloredo to leave at once, he gave a lame excuse. The archbishop had almost certainly been intercepting Wolfgang's rebellious letters; twice already he had spoken 'insulting' words to his court organist. He now flared up, called Mozart 'rascal' and 'dissolute fellow', showed him the door, and told him to clear out. Mozart took this as his dismissal; 'I hate the archbishop to madness.' Count Arco, though, would not accept his letters of resignation, perhaps because his talent still seemed worth holding onto. At the fifth time of asking he called Mozart 'clown' and 'knave' and literally kicked him out.

Mozart was at once furious and relieved. He blustered that he would return the kick with interest, but it signalled to him that the whole ghastly business was over – even though he appears never to have been formally dismissed. By mid-June 1781 he was on his own in Vienna.

Leopold as usual came down (by letter) in massive self-pitying reproach. His son was pursuing pleasure only; his own job might be at risk; he opened a campaign against the Weber influence; it irked him that the money promised failed to arrive. Wolfgang, however, stood his ground. He still, like a dutiful son, answered all the objections in detail, but he wrote firmly that his honour was at stake: 'I can never abandon my resolve.' Leopold seems in time to have acquiesced (his letters of these months are missing, probably destroyed). There was yet to be a prolonged battle over his son's wish to marry Constanze Weber, something an eighteenth-century father must try to control; the father lost, and Wolfgang and Constanze were married on 4 August 1782. Already in summer 1781, however, Wolfgang's career was out of his father's hands.

For that career Vienna held out great promise. Its aristocracy, a sizeable group drawn from all over the Habsburg lands, were highly musical; many, right up to the imperial family, played an instrument; Viennese orchestras were famous for their attack and accurate intonation. The middle-class audience, however, was small, and – as Count Arco warned Mozart in a conversation held before the notorious final one – 'after a few months the Viennese want something new'. True,

Mozart countered, but 'only in the theatre'; as keyboard virtuoso he would in any case last 'a few years' – a good prophecy.

His send-off was indeed to have been in the theatre, with the German comic opera *The Abduction from the Seraglio*. It was held up until 16 July 1782, and its success probably led Mozart to take the plunge and marry Constanze Weber not three weeks later against his family's wishes, as that of *Idomeneo* had led him to skip Colloredo's service. Opera would be a constant aim, now and then fulfilled. The staple of his early Vienna years, however, was his career at the piano. He pursued it in three ways: by appearing at public concerts run either by himself or by fellow artists, where he played his own compositions; by performing them in – mainly aristocratic – private houses; and by giving lessons.

His instrument was the fortepiano, a sound we can now hear again after two hundred years. It needs a hall of moderate size and an orchestra that will not drown it. These conditions were the Viennese norm, even in the Burgtheater, the leading playhouse where Mozart gave concerts, or the Mehlgrube ('Flour Store'), a hall where he arranged subscription series; other rooms were yet more intimate. Mozart virtually invented the piano concerto and, together with C. P. E. Bach, Haydn, and several minor German and Italian composers, launched the piano sonata; but although we can now hear performances on period instruments, we still have to unlearn the sound nineteenth-century composers have taught us to expect from these forms, and desert the halls built for them, if we are to hear the musical events in his works as the original audience did.

Those events were highly dramatic, above all in his improvisations. Most are lost, but he now and then wrote them down. They were not necessarily anguished, like the fantasia in C minor of 1785 (K. 475), which anticipates the Romantics in its lone wanderings about the universe. They could be brilliant or even cheeky, as in certain movements of the sonatas written for Munich in 1774–75 (K. 279–84), and in the outer movements of the two Mannheim sonatas of 1777–78 (K. 309 and 311); in K. 309 the master improviser shows not just in the fireworks but in the quiet, concise ending. For Vienna Mozart wrote, probably in 1783, a further set (K. 330–3), now among his best known works; it includes the specially lovable K. 330 in C, where the shadows (excursions into the minor) in the Andante cantabile lead to the song-like opening tune and skipping happiness of the final Allegretto, as well as the brilliant 'Turkish' concluding rondo of K. 331. Improvisation (of ornaments and cadenzas) was essential to the piano concertos too; they were so bound up with Mozart as performer that he withheld most of them from publication.

These concertos might be called Mozart's crowning achievement if he did not wear several other crowns. The royal line begins at Salzburg in 1773 with the concerto in D (K. 175). With its trumpets and drums it gave both a note of triumph (characteristically shadowed) and opportunities for display. In Vienna Mozart revived it, with a new last movement (the rondo, K. 382) to meet the local taste for jollity. He may also have played the concerto in E♭ for Mlle Jeunehomme, the more inwardly triumphant and inventive K. 271. He then wrote new concertos, fifteen of them in 1782–86, every one a masterpiece.

His aim in the first three of these (K. 413–15), as he told his father, was:

> a happy medium between what is too easy and too difficult; they are
> very brilliant, pleasing to the ear, and natural, without being vapid.
> There are passages here and there from which the connoisseurs
> alone can derive satisfaction; but these passages are written in such
> a way that the less learned cannot fail to be pleased, though without
> knowing why.

He later faced the Viennese with the dark, passionate concertos in D minor and C minor (K. 466 and 491), a long way from the 'happy medium'. The last of the main series, that in C (K. 503), has been described by Joseph Kerman as a 'monumental, rather forbiddingly magnificent' work, signalling 'loss of heart'; by December 1786, Kerman thinks, Mozart may have tired of the Viennese audience. The more usual account is that the audience had tired of Mozart; both may be true. In the remaining five years of his life he wrote only two piano concertos.

Rather than a struggle – Kerman argues in his illuminating essay – the concertos embody a dialogue. Piano and orchestra answer each other in modified versions of the main theme, the piano breaks out into virtuosity, the orchestra – except in the two dark minor-key works – re-establishes consensus in aid of 'play' and of a happy ending. We are at a vernal comedy whose actors learn to understand their own human nature: 'the individual is incorporated into society and society is transformed'.

In Vienna, Mozart the composer-virtuoso quickly won success. Lent, when – before 1788 – the opera closed, was the busiest season. Between 22 February and 4 April 1783 he gave twenty-two concerts; for three of them he had 153 subscribers, mainly nobles; two more were held in the palaces of the grand families Galitzin and Esterhazy; he was giving two concerts a year in the Burgtheater. By February–March 1785 he was able to give six subscription concerts; ten other concerts are documented, and he may have played at several more; his piano was continually being moved out to the theatre or to some private house. He could also afford a handsome flat the rent of which slightly exceeded his old salary from the archbishop. His pupils included at least one, Barbara Ployer, fit to have two of his most iridescent concertos (K. 449 and 453) written for her. He had arrived.

Success of this kind, however, would have been precarious even if he had managed his affairs more carefully; he was in debt by February 1783, when he was busiest. Concert-giving might fail, as it eventually did. Mozart had appreciative, cultivated patrons among the great – Countess Thun, the leading Minister Prince Kaunitz, the imperial librarian and educational administrator Baron Gottfried van Swieten, who introduced him to the music of Johann Sebastian Bach and Handel – but they did not maintain composers. What he really needed, he was aware, was a job in the imperial household.

Characteristically, he would not ask for one. He met the approachable Joseph II and talked to him early in 1782; in spring 1783 Joseph attended one of his concerts, called out 'Bravo Mozart!', waved his hat, and applauded so enthusiastically that – Mozart commented – he would have had to send a present bigger than twenty-five ducats (112 florins) if he had not thoughtfully sent that amount beforehand. No job followed, though. Mozart started to talk of going again to Paris, perhaps to London. No job did come his way until December 1787, when Joseph in person appointed him chamber musician at 800 florins a year. This was less than one-fifth the salary offered that year to the prima donna at the Burgtheater – a normal ratio at the time between a composer's and a star singer's fee. The post was, however, a virtual sinecure with no duties other than to supply some minuets and German dances for court balls.

Joseph's motives can be arrived at indirectly. He thought well of Mozart: according to an official document that did away with the sinecure after both his and Mozart's deaths, he had given it merely to keep 'so rare a genius' in Vienna. He took a close interest in opera; though he would not have serious opera, the grandest and most expensive form, his decisions gave Mozart the chance to compose or revive four of his greatest works, and he directly commissioned the squib The Impresario. His new wind band encouraged Mozart to write three extraordinary wind serenades, and to develop the scoring for winds in his concertos and operas.

Joseph none the less shared the common view that Mozart's music was too learned and complex – in opera, as he wrote, 'too difficult for the singers'. This renders plausible the story that after The Abduction from the Seraglio he said 'Too beautiful for our [Viennese] ears, dear Mozart, and monstrous many notes!' What he preferred was what many others preferred – music by Italians who cultivated simplicity and put the voice first. The composer highest paid and most often performed by Joseph's opera company was Giovanni Paisiello; the Vienna-based composer he relied on most was Antonio Salieri. Both were among the leading composers of the day: to single out their

8   Joseph II and his brother Peter Leopold, later Leopold II: oil painting by
Pompeo Batoni

works was to go along with prevailing taste. Mozart's were special, at
times difficult. Whether Joseph, like other rulers, detected in the
young musician a vein of insubordination we do not know. He shared
Mozart's dislike of pomp; he tried not to mind criticism; his will must

none the less prevail. At any rate he saw high value in Mozart and sub-sidised it, short of a full-time job.

Mozart's Freemasonry was no obstacle. He became a Mason in December 1784, at a time when Masons in Vienna included leading nobles, upper clergy, and government officials as well as two of Mozart's publishers and his sometime landlord, a printer, owner of a hall where he played. Radicals among them supported Joseph in the measures he took to dissolve religious orders, promote toleration, and bring about universal schooling. Mozart set three Masonic texts in praise of Joseph's wisdom. The emperor himself, though, had reservations about Freemasonry. Its ritual struck him as 'mumbo-jumbo'; he disliked its secrecy and its international ties, and thought some Masons dabbled in intrigue. Above all, Freemasonry was a growing organism beyond the control of the state. In December 1785 Joseph cut down the number of lodges and had a register drawn up of their members. The reorganised lodges carried on, and so did their praise – set by Mozart – of Joseph as father and benefactor.

The political climate in Vienna was to turn sour in late 1787, because of the revolution in the Austrian Netherlands (Belgium), itself a forerunner of the French Revolution. Meanwhile, in the mid-1780s, a spirit we might today call 'radical chic' was common among the upper classes, as it was elsewhere in Europe. In the theatre it informed two opera librettos, G. B. Casti's *King Theodore in Venice*, a satire on royalty (Vienna, 1784; music by Paisiello), and Giovanni Bertati's *The Peasant Girl Kidnapped* (*La villanella rapita*, for whose Vienna production in 1785 Mozart wrote two extra numbers); among spoken plays, famously, Beaumarchais's *The Marriage of Figaro*, which Mozart in 1786 was to turn into an evergreen opera.

Beaumarchais's comedy of intrigue, like *La villanella*, denounced aristocratic bullying, in particular the sexual harassment of young plebeian women; it showed a nobleman defeated by the spirit and ingenuity of the lower classes. Figaro's long soliloquy set the career of that plebeian jack-of-all-trades, his talents baffled at every turn by privilege, against the easy life of his master the count, who had 'merely taken the trouble to be born'. This line, close to some of Mozart's remarks, went round Europe.

Censorship in Paris had none the less held up the play for three years until its successful first night in 1784. In Vienna the emperor banned it, but was intelligent enough to realise that a comic opera based on it would meet public interest while leaving out the more subversive bits. As the librettist wrote – the Figaro-like adventurer Lorenzo Da Ponte – an opera drawn from so complicated a work must be an 'extract': apart from the 'prudent considerations' he also referred to, no words for singing could have run to the sheer information in Figaro's soliloquy. Just to make sure, Da Ponte turned it into a comic diatribe against women. The libretto none the less keeps to the main outline of the original story; it still, therefore, shows an arrogant noble humiliated by those he took to be his inferiors – servants, women, adolescents.

In Vienna *Figaro* was a fair rather than an overwhelming success; though Mozart achieved more performances of this and other operas than did fellow German composers, Italians did far better. Like other works of his it drew the usual complaints that it was too richly scored and you could not hum the tunes. There is, however, no evidence that – as has been claimed – it put Viennese aristocrats off Mozart: it was to have more performances in 1789, and again in 1790, than in 1786.

Was it revolutionary? At the time of its first performance in 1786 the French, and for that matter the Netherlands, revolutions had not yet happened; no one was aware of what they might bring. American independence – proclaimed ten years earlier – was, to radicals, inspiring but far off. Modern work on French history shows that it is no use billing *Figaro* as a herald of bourgeois revolution, because the revolution was not made by bourgeois in the Marxian sense of capitalist entrepreneurs: it was made by lawyers, officials, printers, journalists, actors, and other professionals who had both worked the old regime and chafed at its many agglomerations of privilege.

Mozart, like Beaumarchais's Figaro a talented professional dependent on the great yet thwarted and irked by them, fitted the model of potential revolutionary – if he had lived in France. In more backward central Europe the conflict with authority meant detesting and leaving one autocrat who was hostile, and trying to find a job under another who was more intelligent and sympathetic. Little divided Colloredo and Joseph II in ideas or policy; but the emperor was prepared to meet Mozart halfway, and showed greater breadth of spirit. Some nobles, too, at once valued the finer points of Mozart's music and joined him in laughing at their own class. Many would stop laughing by 1792–93, when the new, democratic French Republic plunged into the Terror; but by then Mozart was dead. What he had thought of the revolution in its early, by comparison moderate stages we do not know.

What did most to free him from authority in its harsher mien – the authority of his father, then the archbishop's – was his power to organise sounds into a structure that would resist time.

Not marble, nor the gilded monuments
Of princes, shall outlive this powerful rhyme

Shakespeare had written in a sonnet addressed to a young friend, himself not far from a prince. Mozart did not put it like that, but this small, excitable, not very healthy young man knew his own worth. Others might sneer, he wrote from Mannheim, 'but they will soon see'. He cannot have endeared himself to a lesser composer, given to unusual key changes, when he demonstrated at the piano that you could write even more unusual ones 'and yet not offend the ear'. To a successful older colleague, Niccolò Piccinni, he was polite but no more: 'I do not seek acquaintanceship, either with him or with any other composer. I understand my job – and so do they – and that is enough.'

It was left to the one composer he utterly respected, Haydn, to define Mozart's status. When he met Leopold Mozart in 1785 he said 'Before God and as an honest man I tell you that your son is the greatest composer known to me either in person or by name. He has taste and, what is more, the most profound knowledge of composition.' There is here a little more than meets the eye. 'Knowledge of composition' meant mastery of all styles, including 'learned' counterpoint,

9   The Michaelerplatz and the Burgtheater, Vienna: engraving by Carl Schütz

and full control of harmony. 'Taste' in the late eighteenth century meant the use of those tools to make an aesthetically satisfying whole. Haydn's praise could not have gone further.

The occasion, a performance at Wolfgang's home during Leopold's one visit to him in Vienna, was fitting: it was of three out of the six string quartets Mozart dedicated to Haydn, the creator of the form as we know it. In dedicating these 'children' of his to the 'great man and my dearest friend', Mozart wrote that the quartets were 'the fruit of long and laborious endeavour'. This was true: he had written them over at least two and a half years (1782–85), with many erasures and false starts. Alfred Einstein called them 'music made of music', 'filtered' art. To the listener they may at times sound, in their calibrated refinement, a shade less spontaneous than others among Mozart's greatest works: the 'endeavour' shows. But they were meant for those who could play their way into them at home; there was then no Wigmore Hall, no Alice Tully Hall, no passive audience for such things; the player would discover them as he or she recreated them, marvelling at the novel chromaticisms and dissonances. Explication now would have to go in detail into every movement, almost every bar. They are what Virginia Woolf called 'the square upon the oblong' – the work achieved and self-sufficient; together with Haydn's quartets they remain the foundation of the string quartet repertoire.

Some works of Mozart's can be found squaring up to authority. The serenade for winds in C minor (K. 388) is one. He probably composed it in 1782, and later (1787–88) rewrote it as a string quintet (K. 406), to try to make up another of his unfinished sets; in the smoother texture it loses some of its bite. We do not know why he wrote it in the first place; its four-movement structure is that of a symphony, and its mood lies as far as it well could from entertainment.

This is public music, all the same. It deals with great, unspecified, alarming events of concern to all. The opening theme, rising and then falling in a diminished seventh, is tense, stringent; the second theme rocks disconsolately, in a version still more troubled when the oboe recapitulates it; sudden cries of distress punctuate the development. The ending of this first Allegro is terse, like the work as a whole. A token of solace in the Andante proves illusory, even within this short movement. The minuet with its sudden dissonances is relentless, even fierce. So is the first of the eight variations in the final Allegro, to a theme that turns round and round on itself; the third variation brings ominous syncopations, the fourth a slightly sinister fair-ground dance; in the next to last, deep disturbance leads to a moment when the theme hesitates and, in Hermann Abert's words, 'appears to fall to pieces'. Only the final variation wins through to positive C major; even it seems to say 'There! Take it or leave it.'

Running through the work, however, is a potentially contradictory use of musical language. It relies a great deal on counterpoint, the more striking because held on a tight rein. The minuet is a canon, the unearthly trio a double mirror canon: Mozart had been listening, at his friend van Swieten's, to J. S. Bach. (He had long had a thorough knowledge of counterpoint, but reading Bach's fugues and canons and holding them under his fingers was a revelation.) Canons and other mathematical forms deck music in an armour of impersonality.

10 The Graben, one of Mozart's many addresses in Vienna: engraving by Carl
Schütz

They open – as they already did in the late eighteenth century – a long
backward view, certainly to Bach, even to the Flemish masters of the
Renaissance. They speak for unchanging truth. The serenade in C
minor is the work of a rebel against the order of things; it holds
menace, almost obsessive and withheld only in a last quick gesture;
yet, like many rebels, its author has deep roots in the traditional order
that maddens him. The resulting tension makes the work at least as
profoundly revolutionary as Beethoven's seventh symphony.

Does the 'Jupiter' symphony hold something of that tension? This
symphony in C (K. 551), is one of the famous set of three that Mozart
composed within a couple of months in the summer of 1788, for an
unknown purpose; he almost certainly had in view a concert series, a
tour, or publication, and very likely heard them played. The 'Jupiter',
Neal Zaslaw has written, may be called revolutionary on grounds not
unlike those just advanced for the C minor serenade. Its first movement mixes noble and comic-plebeian elements; the Andante
cantabile gives a sense of repeated tension, negation, and unease;
chromaticism in the minuet denies the traditional dance character of

the form; the last movement permutates five themes and then combines them in the coda to make a fugato in five-part invertible counterpoint, with a sixth theme coming in (after a brief glance back at Leopold Mozart's world) to resolve the conflict in powerful homophony.

Zaslaw's analysis is plausible, yet his question – may we not perhaps glimpse Mozart here 'dreaming of escaping his oppressive past and giving utterance to his fondest hopes and highest aspirations for the future'? – makes him sound too much like Elgar. Mozart is more rigorous than that. There is in the 'Jupiter' no sense of 'interesting', unresolved personal problems, no likely reference to outward events.

The first movement does set up an opposition between a triumphant 'noble' theme and a gracious 'comic opera' theme, but – after the Harlequins have gone, in the development, through modulations doubtful, searching, even aggressive – the movement ends in unclouded health. The slow movement's passing minor-mode effusion, troubled appoggiaturas, and weird key change at the climax of a series of modulations likewise give way to the suavity that began it. The minuet gives out a powerful self-confidence, briefly qualified by the plaintive cadence that opens the trio. Self-confidence – powerful, joyous, triumphant – is again the note of the finale. Trumpets and drums cheer it on its way; it is from the start elaborately contrapuntal, yet the counterpoint, with the almost grinding dissonances it sets up before the end, is wholly absorbed in an exhilarating tour de force. 'Can he do it, will he do it?' – we never ask that, the mastery is so plain.

If the 'Jupiter' is revolutionary, it is music for an ideal revolution that could happen only in the spirit. Mozart here takes the inner conflict with authority by the scruff of the neck; he dissolves and resolves it in music – for himself and for us.

3 The eternal feminine

In Venice the fifteen-year-old Mozart and his father saw a lot of a German family whose six beautiful daughters were known as the 'pearls'. The 'pearls' and their mother tried – as Wolfgang told Nannerl – to make a 'true Venetian' of him by getting him down on the floor and spanking his bottom, but 'they could not pull me down'. This little incident of February 1771 sets the erotic tone for Mozart's career as both man and artist: girt about with delightful women, holding a chance of perversity or tears, but in the end comic.

Comedy is much more than something to laugh at and forget. It is, according to Wye J. Allanbrook, the organising model of Mozart's work: a 'cosmic mirror that presents all species of things in their compelling diversity, and affirms their integration . . . into an overarching communal hierarchy'. Another way to put it might be: for Mozart all men and women ultimately play their part in the created world, whatever grief or peril may threaten them at times, and that part is at once joyous and right. Love, our most serious concern, properly ends in laughter.

The eighteenth century, for much of its length, was an age of eroticism understood as comedy. We see this in the painting of Tiepolo, Boucher, and Fragonard: a light palette combines with airy views; in painting faces, the artist differentiates them very little by sex (most men of the age were clean shaven), though the bodies may be voluptuous and the moment shown suggestive. In the writings of Sterne and

Diderot the erotic may veer off into pathos on the one hand, near-pornography on the other, but the Eros who presides is in the end a reasonable, smiling god. True, from the 1760s people began to welcome images of the erotic as passion and despair hurtling, maybe, to suicide; but although Mozart was eighteen when Goethe's *The Sorrows of Young Werther* came out in 1774, his life and work brought to a last flower the earlier age of sensibility, of the erotic as, at worst, tears ending in reconciliation and joy.

In its actuality the century was a time for adventurers. The new ease of upper-class life made possible careers summed up in that of Casanova; another, only slightly less hectic, was that of Lorenzo Da Ponte, the librettist of Mozart's finest Italian comic operas. What kind of erotic life most people led, and how they experienced it, is almost wholly beyond our knowing. So with Mozart and his experience of women. We know a little about his relationship with his mother (dependent) and his sister (jocular), a little more about his married life, hardly anything about what he otherwise made of love and sex.

This has not stopped rumour-mongers, then or now. Nothing provokes gossip – fast veering into assertion – so much as other people's erotic lives. When a great artist dies at thirty-five, the brakes are off. Eyewitnesses and early biographers talked of Mozart's 'weaknesses', 'human failings', 'hazardous' contacts, and 'debaucheries'. What did they mean? They did not say; many interpretations are possible. For the modern biographer Maynard Solomon such hints, together with gaps and oddities in Mozart's letters, make it exceedingly likely that he was unfaithful to his wife during his tour to Berlin in 1789. The evidence, however, bears no such weight if tested by ordinary historical methods, let alone by those of a divorce court. We do not know whether Mozart was unfaithful. Why not admit it, and move on?

We are left with impressions. 'If I had to marry all those with whom I have jested', the twenty-five-year-old bachelor told his father, 'I should have two hundred wives at least.' He wrote to deny – perhaps untruthfully – any serious entanglement with Constanze Weber, so this may have been special pleading. On the other hand his letters suggest that the unmarried Mozart was continually in love with some young woman, and that until he met the Webers love was much taken up with 'jesting' – little documented but perhaps not so crude as the exchanges with his cousin Maria Thekla. When newly married, he could write a mock love letter to a noble patron, Baroness Waldstätten – a separated woman who would once have been described as 'fast': 'since the night when I saw your Ladyship at the ball with your hair so beautifully dressed . . . gone is my peace of mind! Nothing but sighs and groans! . . . But alas! Who taps me on the shoulder? Who peeps into my letter? Alas, alas, alas! My wife!' We can see both the smile on Mozart's face and the one he meant to raise on the Baroness's.

He, his wife, and many of his friends and acquaintances were members of theatrical professions: he shared in theatre people's camaraderie and flirtatiousness. At the same time he described himself, in letters to his father, as a 'clean-minded' young man of good family, who would not keep a mistress or deal with loose women. This we may perhaps discount, but his later correspondence with his wife shows that he did mind about his own 'honour', something her behaviour in public might jeopardise. That honour might suffer because of his own conduct does not appear: Mozart, more sympathetic to women than the bulk of his contemporaries, shared their double standard. At twenty-one he could sign himself 'Knight of the Golden Spur and, as soon as I marry, of the Double Horn'. Cuckoldry worked only one way; in his opera scores the horn does punning duty, commenting on the plight of men betrayed by women.

The first woman he loved in more than a 'jesting' or passing way was almost certainly Aloisia Weber. They met at Mannheim in the autumn of 1777, when he was twenty-one and she, probably, sixteen. The next was Aloisia's sister Constanze, nineteen years old in 1781, when she and the twenty-five-year-old Mozart met again in Vienna. The facts that so appalled Leopold Mozart are straightforward enough, widely though their interpretation can vary.

Aloisia at first returned Wolfgang's love and enchanted him with her singing. In September 1778 she and her father won appointments in Munich that made them financially comfortable; by Christmas Wolfgang found that she no longer loved him; in 1780 she married the actor and painter Joseph Lange. For young people to fall in and out of love is so common that we need not think her mercenary. By May 1781 in Vienna, when Mozart was lodging with the Webers, he admitted 'I was a fool . . . but what does not a man do when he is in love?' Aloisia was 'still not a matter of indifference to me'. He may already have been in love with Constanze, but – again – it is common enough for a young person to keep a soft spot for the old love while getting on with the new.

To his father he denied the new love but admitted (in July 1781) that he might have to move out of the Webers' flat because his presence had given rise to gossip; at most he owned to 'fooling about' with Constanze. He was, he said, reluctant to move because at the Webers' he could work and eat in his dressing gown, and meal times were rearranged to suit him – an artist's paradise. Leopold, however, clearly insisted that he should move out, and, in August, he did.

Only in December 1781 did Mozart admit that he was in love with Constanze and wished to marry her. Furthermore, the widowed Frau Weber and the children's legal guardian had obliged him, on pain of no longer seeing Constanze, to promise in writing that he would either marry her within three years or, if he did not, would pay her an income of 300 florins. Constanze, however, had torn up the paper.

Leopold's furious response was that Frau Weber and the guardian were 'seducers of youth' who had entrapped his son and should be put in chains. Wolfgang denied this roundly. He was, none the less, ambivalent about Frau Weber: at one time he saw her as a hostile parent from whom Constanze had to be 'rescued', and Constanze did move out to stay with Baroness Waldstätten, the somewhat 'fast' noblewoman already mentioned (her mother, it seems, threatened to have her brought back by the police). Mozart and Frau Weber were none the less reconciled by the time he married Constanze on 4 August 1782, all those present weeping tears of joy. Leopold's blessing, which he gave reluctantly after many strong objections, arrived the next day.

11   Constanze Weber: oil painting by her brother-in-law Joseph Lange

The parents' attitude calls for historical explanation. Frau Weber, as a widow of small means with unmarried daughters, living on the fringe of the theatrical profession, had to maintain a precarious respectability. The unmarried daughters might all too easily fall prey to a seducer and then be dragged down into poverty, even into prostitution. Extracting a written promise of marriage was a defensive measure. That was the basic situation; what else caused the temporary breach between mother and daughter we do not know.

Leopold and Nannerl – she objected to the marriage as much as he did, and kept it up far longer – had different family prospects to think of. The Salzburg Mozarts were a 'middling' family with at its head a man who had climbed, in education and local standing, well past his brothers and sisters. The one surviving son was a genius who should be able to win an official post conferring honour as well as money. He ought to marry a woman at least his social equal, who would bring a dowry. The family would then be on its way to a secure place in the world, perhaps to land ownership and ennoblement. They would be safe from the perils that lay in wait at a time when illness or misfortune struck down many, leaving them to their own resources. Instead the genius son married an ill-educated, penniless young woman from a family at once grasping and doubtfully respectable, two of whose other daughters were on the stage. He put his own pleasure ahead of his family's well-being. What Leopold wrote to his son in the crucial months is lost, but these – Wolfgang's replies suggest – were his arguments. They were wholly in line with the normal expectations of 'middling' families, though Leopold no doubt added his own touch of pedantry and self-pity.

Nannerl, for her part, was to do the expected thing by marrying, two years after Wolfgang, a local nobleman with children by two previous wives. He was forty-eight, she thirty-three, so they were not ill-matched according to the view of the time. Whether the marriage was happy we can scarcely tell. Nannerl, at all events, disliked her brother's marriage and what it did to the family enough to tell a biographer, after Wolfgang's death, that on all matters after 1781 (down to her sister-in-law's name) he should inquire in Vienna.

Mozart's own attitude was in stark contrast. It was modern – for 1781–82, advanced. While he was in love with Aloisia he had told his father – seemingly apropos of another couple – that he would not wish to marry for money: all he wanted was 'to make my wife happy'. In

December 1781, when he declared himself to Leopold, he wrote plainly:

> The voice of nature speaks as loud in me as in others, louder, perhaps, than in many a big strong lout of a fellow. I simply cannot live as most young men do in these days. In the first place, I have too much religion; in the second place, I have too great a love of my neighbour and too high a feeling of honour to seduce an innocent girl; and, in the third place, I have too much horror and disgust, too much dread and fear of diseases and too much care for my health to fool about with whores.

He also needed a wife to help him with everyday needs: 'a bachelor... is only half alive'. In Constanze he had found 'the kindest-hearted, the cleverest and, in short, the best' of the Weber sisters, the pillar of the household yet a martyr to the rest. About her other qualities he was realistic:

> She is not ugly, but at the same time far from beautiful. Her whole beauty consists in two little black eyes and a pretty figure. She has no wit, but she has enough common sense to enable her to fulfil her duties as a wife and mother. It is a downright lie that she is inclined to be extravagant... she understands housekeeping and has the kindest heart in the world. I love her and she loves me with all her heart. Tell me whether I could wish myself a better wife?

At first his marriage was to wait on his getting a fixed income; but just as Mozart's achievement with *Idomeneo* had nerved him to resign from Colloredo's service, so his Viennese success with *The Abduction from the Seraglio* freed him to marry Constanze nineteen days later. He still pleaded for his father's consent – arguing that he had gone too far to withdraw – but was ready to anticipate it. 'We are made for each other', he wrote afterwards, 'and God, who orders all things and consequently has ordered this also, will not forsake us.' In letters to Salzburg he and Constanze signed jointly; 'man and wife', one letter ended, 'are one life'.

Leopold was realist enough to accept Constanze, though he went on speaking ill of her family – probably the reason why his letters to his son are missing after as well as before the wedding: Constanze no doubt burnt them. To Baroness Waldstätten he wrote with his usual acumen, and with unusual detachment, about his son's impracticality – all the more worrying because 'it is unfortunately . . . those who possess outstanding genius who have the greatest obstacles to face . . . My dear lady, please instil a little patience into my son.'

The newly married couple were to have visited Salzburg almost at once, but obstacles came up – bad weather, the busy concert season, Constanze's pregnancy. These were real enough, though as the time to go drew near Mozart speculated – needlessly – that in Salzburg the archbishop might have him arrested. In the event he and Constanze spent the three months August–October 1783 at his father's. Some late, indirect evidence hints that relations were strained – perhaps with Nannerl, for when Leopold in turn visited the young Mozarts in Vienna, from February to April 1785, they seem to have got on and he praised his daughter-in-law's 'economical' housekeeping. The one known result of the Salzburg visit was Mozart's great, unfinished Mass in C minor (K. 427), written, it appears, as a thank-offering for his wife's safe delivery and performed, with Constanze as soloist, in the great abbey church of St Peter's.

The notion that the visit estranged the Salzburg and the Vienna Mozarts is a latter-day misunderstanding. To Leopold and Nannerl the marriage came as a blow, but relations were kept up, the family tie prevailed; Wolfgang wrote his sister a lightly bawdy verse letter on her wedding. If correspondence grew sparser and dealt with professional more than with personal matters, that was a normal consequence of Wolfgang's having – in the legal language of the time – emancipated himself. He had set up an independent household, he and Leopold were no longer directly responsible for and to each other. Wolfgang's repeated excuse for answering late – he had been frantically busy – was both true and an unsurprising token that as a mature husband and father he was growing away from the Mozart family cocoon.

What sort of a husband he made, and how Constanze turned out as a wife, divides opinion. A straightforward reading of his letters to her suggests that the marriage was happy and sexually fulfilled. His occasional concern, both before and after the wedding, at her letting down his 'honour' by tolerating indiscretions and not minding appearances – famously, by allowing a young man-about-town to measure her calves – suggests that he was, as usual, in two minds about the theatre world he mixed in. On the one hand he found that world congenial, had indeed married into it; his and Constanze's playing hide-and-seek, when he lodged at the Webers', with a woman who later turned up married to an actor suggests a little-documented side of his life. On the other hand he was touchy about his standing as a respectable citizen and a man of 'honour' who had mixed freely with the great; the measuring of his fiancée's calves in a parlour game stood for all that put him off theatre manners.

A letter written in 1789, when Constanze was getting over an illness at a spa outside Vienna, suggests both that she was at that moment caught up in 'unnecessary jealousy' and that Wolfgang was upset at her having been 'free and easy' with two men on two separate occasions. Only conjecture allows one to think this much more than a passing discord in married life.

'Your dear little kissable arse', Mozart wrote to her that same year on one of the few trips he took without her (promising a spanking if she really thought he had forgotten her); in his hotel room he would address her portrait: 'Good day, little rascal, pussy-pussy, little turned-up nose, little bagatelle . . . Good night, little mouse, sleep well.' Another letter, announcing his return, she kept but blotted out words in strategic places:

> Arrange your dear sweet nest very daintily, for my little fellow deserves it indeed, he has really behaved himself very well and is only longing to possess your sweetest [blot]. Just picture to yourself that rascal; as I write he crawls on to the table and looks at me questioningly. I, however, box his ears – but the rogue is simply [blot] and now the knave burns only more fiercely and can hardly be restrained.

12 Daniel Nikolaus Chodowiecki, 'The artist's daughter at her mother's breast'. This tender drawing of 1761 suggests the enthusiasm for breastfeeding which Rousseau instilled into some upper-class mothers. Not, however, into the Mozarts, some of whose children died after having been put out in risky traditional fashion to a wet-nurse.

A good sexual relationship meant, at the time, repeated pregnancies. In nine years' married life Constanze gave birth to six children, of whom only the second and the last, Karl Thomas and Franz Xaver Wolfgang, lived more than a few months (as adults they were to pursue respectably mediocre careers); some died within hours.

This side of the Mozarts' life is almost wholly veiled. After the birth of the eldest child, Raimund Leopold, in 1783 Mozart wrote that he 'is quite strong and healthy and has a tremendous number of things to do, I mean, drinking, sleeping, yelling, pissing, shitting, dribbling, and so forth. He kisses the hands of his grandpapa and his aunt.' After his death at two months – Wolfgang and Constanze, Salzburg bound, had left him with a wet-nurse, a normal step at the time for parents of their class – both were 'very sad about our poor, bonny, fat, darling little boy.' That the deaths of later children passed without mention in surviving letters tells us nothing. Mozart went to some trouble over Karl's schooling and, as one of his last acts before the illness that killed him, took the seven-year-old boy to a performance of *The Magic Flute*.

Through those nine years' married life Wolfgang and Constanze shared ten different lodgings. By far the grandest of these (at an annual rent greater than Mozart's former salary of 450 florins) lasted them two and half years, from September 1784 to April 1787; they occupied their last dwelling for nearly three years, so their average stay in the remaining eight was just over seven months.

Such mobility was not as odd as it now looks. People other than the very rich had, by our standards, few belongings; manual labour was cheap, and rented housing not hard to find; it was correspondingly easier to move. Theatre people, with whom the Mozarts had a good deal in common, were used to frequent moves. They were also used to a feast-and-famine existence: Wolfgang and Constanze moved at least twice on financial grounds – to a suburban lodging because they could no longer afford a flat in town; they moved back into the centre when things picked up. The fine dwelling they expanded into in September 1784 went with Mozart's peak period of success as concert giver, just as a flat yet more expensive went with the success of his friend and librettist, the playwright Gottlieb Stephanie; Leopold, on his visit, marvelled at such lavishness (and at the high Viennese rent), but by 1787 it was all too much to cope with.

Mozart's finances have caused much ink to flow. Some writers have made strenuous efforts to estimate his income and expenditure in Vienna. The trouble is, first, that we know only in part the activities from which Mozart drew an income (and still less the items on which he spent money); secondly, that even for some of these we have to form estimates, based on what someone at the time reported the usual fee to be for a particular kind of appearance by a musician. Such reports, as other contemporary evidence shows, can inflate the amounts paid; it is best to stick to detailed accounts – of payments made by official bodies or noble households, for example – fragmentary though they may be. Mozart's own reports of what he was paid cannot be taken on trust. As was said of Desdemona, 'she has deceiv'd her father, and may thee'; unlike her, Mozart may not have stopped deceiving once he left his father's house. Precise totals of income and expenditure may therefore mislead.

The basic problem is none the less clear. In his best Vienna years, down to 1787, Mozart as independent composer-performer earned a sizeable income, probably somewhere around 2,000 to 3,000 florins a year, in the main from concert appearances in public and in private; fees from opera managements, from music publishers, and from pupils made up the rest, together with the odd windfall, like the sale of various pieces of music to a South German ruling prince. By late nineteenth-century standards fees were low, and copyright non-existent, so that repeat productions of operas, for instance, would bring in nothing; the cost of living in Vienna, too, was much higher than at Salzburg. This tells us only that it was difficult for an eighteenth-century composer to save and grow rich: though Mozart's estimated income would not have brought wealth, it should have been enough to support him and his family in some style and leave him reasonably free from care. Nevertheless – the earliest evidence dates from February 1783, six months after the wedding – Mozart frequently borrowed money, often in a hurry and pleading urgent need. The crisis in his finances was to come later, in 1788–90. Meanwhile, how did his handling of them affect his married life?

To be in debt was, at the time, normal. Even rich aristocrats might have trouble laying hands on cash; payment was often late. People might – as Mozart did on occasion – lend money to one friend while themselves in debt to another. Until 1787 there is no clear evidence that Mozart's borrowings were other than this kind of short-term expedient. Leopold, visiting Vienna in the midst of his son's busy and profitable concert season of Lent 1785, thought Wolfgang could lodge 2,000 florins in the bank, though he added, significantly, 'if [he] *has no debts to pay*'; the money, he told Nannerl, 'is certainly there, and so far as eating and drinking is concerned, the housekeeping is extremely economical'. This, from a man as shrewd and precise as Leopold, suggests a large cash flow, but also, perhaps, outstanding debts and heavy expenditure on items other than food and drink.

What might those items be? Mozart loved fine clothes and, by mixing with the great, had developed aristocratic tastes. These may account for a high, in the end unsustainable level of expenditure, but perhaps not for sudden, repeated borrowings of amounts large and small.

A few scholars have inferred that Mozart was a gambler. For this there is no direct evidence. It would, all the same, plausibly account for his known behaviour. A gambling habit typically brings sudden financial ups and downs; the downs can be abysmal and call for urgent remedies. It can also explain why a man who earns a lot of money is at times flat broke. If Mozart was such a man, we need not imagine him in some Viennese gambling den. He liked to play billiards; all he had to do was bet substantial sums on his own game and others'. Gambling was so common in eighteenth-century society that his might pass without remark, other than the talk of 'human failings' and 'hazardous' company that followed his death.

This possibility – it is no more than that – raises the suspicion that Mozart's frequent reports of low earnings on his concert tours masked his gambling losses. These reports – first to Leopold, then to Constanze – accompanied his tours of 1777–79, 1789, and 1790, when he was on his own for much of the time and spent hours or days at a loose end. He was apparently willing to misstate his earnings the other way when it suited him: in December 1789 he told his friend and long-suffering creditor Michael Puchberg, from whom he urgently wished to borrow 400 florins, that he would soon collect a fee for *Così fan tutte* of 900 florins, but the imperial accounts show only a payment of the standard fee for an opera of 450 florins. Charitable scholars suggest that Mozart may have been paid the rest privately by Joseph II, or that Joseph's illness and death may have stopped payment. A more straightforward explanation is that Mozart, in a tight corner, lied to his friend.

What Constanze made of her husband's gambling habit (if it existed) or his poor financial management (which is beyond doubt) we do not know. Her own management of the estate after his death was steady and competent. She soon cleared the debts – already cut down by the rise in Mozart's fortunes in the last year of his life – eventually married a former diplomat, and lived in quiet comfort until her own death more than fifty years later, in 1842. We need not, perhaps, think that during her years with Mozart she was often in despair at their financial troubles. These were never so hopeless that they had to do without a servant or go short of food. She and Wolfgang were both artists, with a background or a strong interest in the theatre and many theatrical friends. In such a milieu, ups and downs of fortune were common; awkward moments need not prevent young people such as the Mozarts from enjoying life and each other or, more especially, from enjoying the upward flight of Wolfgang's art.

In the best of the Vienna years, running from *The Abduction from the Seraglio* in July 1782 to *The Marriage of Figaro* in May 1786, that flight took wing chiefly in his piano concertos. It is not by chance that two opera titles frame a statement about the royal line of Vienna concertos (only K. 413–15 and K. 503 fall outside those dates, by a few months). Mozart, a composer made for opera who wanted nothing so much as to write one, had no other theatre commissions in those years but for the one-act squib *The Impresario*. For him the piano concerto was, amid much else, a continuation of opera by other means.

The high point in *Seraglio* – the quartet for the two pairs of lovers that closes the second act – looks forward to the emotional adventure that in one way and another shapes the finest concertos. It runs through four movements, each coloured by a dominant feeling. In the first the two pairs in turn sing – to different themes – of their joy at being reunited in the perilous surroundings of the seraglio where the women have been shut up, then, together, sing a third melody, here and there shaded ('Voll entzücken'). A change of key and rhythm in the second section has the men questioning whether the women's virtue has held out; the discord this brings takes the music through regions strange and ominous, until Blonde slaps Pedrillo; to a new theme the men beg forgiveness; as all sing together, further modulations and sour harmony tell of dispersion and anguish, until (the women's unreconciled words notwithstanding) a second tutti restores a chorale-like peace. The third section opens with Pedrillo's swinging new theme and goes on to the women's forgiveness; the last ('Es lebe die Liebe') makes a fast, brilliant send-off though with a characteristic passing shadow.

What Mozart could do at this operatic high point he could do, with almost unending versatility, in the piano concertos that followed. Listeners have long noted the singing style of much of the piano music, above all in the slow movements (often compared to arias) but not only there.

Song, in or out of the theatre, gives voice to human emotion, often to that of love in all its shadings; it speaks – as was said at the time of a passage in one of the concertos – 'the language of the heart'. True, Mozart wrote the concertos to exploit his own virtuoso performance; though the virtuosity entailed calls for depth of musical understanding far more than for keyboard gymnastics, in that sense they are, like opera, public music. Yet they are also intimate: as Einstein wrote, the concerto in Mozart's hands 'always leaves the door open to the expression of the darkest and the brightest, the most serious, the gayest, the deepest feelings'.

Where did those feelings spring from? It is idle to think that a composer writes a melancholy tune because an event in his life has just then saddened him. The creative imagination does not work like that. Mozart could write happy music when in deep trouble; he could also compose while his wife was giving birth in the next room. Nor, however, does the creative imagination work out of touch with the artist's inner life. That touch may be oblique, delayed, anticipatory, transmuting; it acts none the less.

In their extraordinary abundance and variety the concertos are the work of a musician who tests the limits of his own powers to create, from symphonic music and the modest pre-existing concerto for keyboard solo and strings, a virtually new form. They are the peak of his instrumental music; as much as *Idomeneo*, they embody his delight in wind instruments and his economical, concealed art in writing for them.

We may, however, also find in the concertos the expression of Mozart's life during those early Vienna years as a young husband and an artist bound for new heights. 'It is one of the perfections' of their music, again in Einstein's words, 'that its dramatic element remains latent, and that it contains more profound depths than the struggle between opposing forces'; piano and orchestra are equals; rather than a conflict, theirs is a 'duality in unity'. This duality (Joseph Kerman's 'dialogue') runs between soloist and players, between stage and auditorium, but also between Mozart's inner being and the created world he experienced in these years with its discoveries joyful, troubling, or delightfully absurd. This we might gloss, in part: 'between him and Constanze'. The concertos are scenes from young married life, triple-distilled.

What goes on in the more intimate of these concerto movements? That different pairs of ears hear different feelings means only that love has many shades. Tenderness may utter in the midst of grief, a shiver of apprehension run athwart felicity. Of all Western music, Mozart's best conveys this emotional freight, light yet profound, many-splendoured yet ambiguous. It does it as a rule by modulation, often touched in by a fleck of wind music.

In the Adagio of the piano concerto in A (K. 488) – a movement itself in F♯ minor, an unusual key for Mozart – one critic hears 'resignation and hopelessness', another 'gentle melancholy', a third a grief shared by two singers from two points of view. The piano's opening stepwise phrases do indeed tell of melancholy love, but we may feel in the answering clarinet melody (over rocking harmony) a touch of solace. The piano repeats its sad song, follows with rising phrases that seem to question; above the rocking harmony it takes over the consolatory tune but quickly subsides; modulations in the winds bring back the original keyboard plaint, now transposed to seem at once hushed and mature; the consolatory melody, repeated, is taken over by the whole orchestra; the piano in stepwise, repeated-note descent acknowledges resignation, then falls to uttering isolated notes – as if it did not trust itself with more – far apart, in vocal leaps, against quiet pizzicato strings. The end is brief restatement and the shortest farewell.

Whatever we hear in this movement – if we hear it at all – the spirit has travelled through regions where deepest love mingles with grief, ventures to hope, withdraws, in the end accepts. Nor is the movement isolated within the concerto. In the first Allegro the bouncy opening theme soon gives way to another which, in its gentle eloquence, speaks of shadows; mystery clusters about the transitional passage that leads to the development, and there, through modulations into keys that sound remoter than they always are, flicks into a passing threat. Dialogue takes over: the winds come in, one instrument or pair at a time, then the piano, then the winds again; we go through alternations of the two main themes and of loud and soft, until the second, shadowed theme, now beset with hesitancies, takes the piano up to the cadenza. Even in the final Allegro assai the gay, rippling piano part – 'shallowness of genius' in Arthur Hutchings's words – meets startled cries of joy and, at one point in the winds, a hint of reserve.

If we take Freud's definition of Eros as the expansive instinct, directed outwards at enjoyment of the created world, the A major concerto is a pervasively erotic work. It runs through a great range of feeling for the earthly other, and fines down in the Adagio to one of the most poignant utterances of love for another human being. Whether the beloved is lost we do not know: what the music speaks for is our apprehension of a loss that may come (has come, will come) and take away our reason for living.

This is true in varying ways of the other concertos, some of them formally more complex than K. 488. The two concertos for Barbara (Babette) Ployer, K. 449 in E♭ and K. 453 in G – both written to a deliberately modest scale, without trumpets and drums, so that she could play them to guests in her own house – show a quicksilver mutability of feeling unusual even for Mozart. The song of tranquil happiness in the Andante of K. 449 comes after a restless Allegro vivace, storm and calm interwoven, then further worried in quick chromatic alternations and juxtapositions; the song discourses, as it goes on, the incidents of a happy life shared, mild crises among them. The 'tears in things' seldom dwell far from the music of K. 453, another work apt to rouse varying emotions in its hearers; flecks of anguish, all the same, never grow extreme or mar the prevailing tenderness; even the final Allegretto (which brings a fanfare-like comic opera coda) has an opening piano theme that is happily discursive. A biographer on the lookout for affairs might think Mozart was in love with his pupil Babette; more likely he felt that her heart could speak his language, while he knew her fingers could deliver pearly runs and arpeggios.

The erotic in its widest sense informs the more outwardly ambitious concertos of this period, even the urbane and brilliant K. 450 in B♭, let alone the more personal K. 467 in C, from the panache of its opening to the triumphant (not unshaded) wit of its ending, with in between the Andante's undulant song, an outpouring of paradisal love over string triplets, their 'heartbeat' sustaining the idyll throughout. In the development of the first Allegro the work discusses matters of serious import: what is personal is also energetically involved with the world; progress through modulations weird and dissonant leads to a maturer, more relaxed statement of the known theme. Such a work is, though less obviously, as much a spiritual autobiography as a tone poem by Richard Strauss.

Mozart, indeed, nearly always speaks in the voice of the individual face to face with the world, a voice intricate with feeling. By the 1780s the impersonality of J. S. Bach, the sense that what rules both the individual and the world is a force deeper than both, was (though he was then studying Bach) no longer available to a Western artist. True, the exceptionally long first movement of the piano concerto in C (K. 503), finished by December 1786 but perhaps started a year or two earlier, may seem impersonal in its complex working of short, not very characterful themes ('strangely cold', as Joseph Kerman writes). Some, though, hear in it an affirmation of the artist's self, so sure (for the moment) of its conquering power that it need no longer enchant. In any event that was the last of the Vienna piano concertos, but for one occasional work and one masterpiece that belongs to Mozart's last phase.

He had by then written *The Marriage of Figaro*. It opened the series of Italian comic operas that was to give Mozart another of his crowns – as author of three works at once sharply funny and mysteriously poetic. Mozart himself saw the making of opera as central to his career; the operas he wrote during his years of success in Munich and Vienna – with *Così fan tutte* a late distillation – stand at the heart of his work. In the inexhaustible joy they have given since their creation Eros plays a large part.

4 Man of the theatre

'I have only to hear an opera discussed, I have only to sit in a theatre, hear the orchestra tuning their instruments – oh, I am quite beside myself at once.' When he wrote this in October 1777 Mozart was on the road in Munich, trying to give concerts and find an established post. What he really wanted was to compose an Italian opera or, better, several – if possible in Italy: 'they would bring me more credit than if I were to give a hundred concerts in Germany'. For a young composer the aim was self-evident: Italian opera was the chief musical genre. The Saxons Handel and Hasse, the Bohemians Gluck and Mysliveček, the Spaniard Martín y Soler were only some of the non-Italian composers who made their mark in it. Mozart hoped to equal them at least.

He was, more than has generally been acknowledged, a man of the theatre. Not only did he wish to write for it; he spent many of his evenings there, taking in both opera and spoken plays, and he knew many theatre people, chief among them his wife's family.

The theatre in his day was both the premier entertainment and the heart of social life – a place it would gradually lose in the nineteenth century. Many educated townspeople went as a matter of course night after night, among them Leopold Mozart and his family when they had the chance. They did not always sit out the performance or attend to all that was happening on stage; they might converse, eat, walk about, or gamble. A scene or a performer must be remarkable for a hush to fall over the house.

The Italian operagoers for whom the adolescent Mozart wrote in 1770–72 would half-listen to a successful work through twenty performances in a row. The more usual practice, for spoken plays everywhere and, in German-speaking lands, for opera as well, was a change of bill every few days. In twelve years' management of a Vienna suburban theatre, Emanuel Schikaneder – librettist, director, and first Papageno of *The Magic Flute* – put on 404 productions, 57 of them his own work (altogether he wrote some one hundred plays). *The Magic Flute* with its forty or so performances in two months was exceptional: most of his productions came off after two or three. A limited audience that dropped in again and again enjoyed a novel touch within an accustomed frame. Like the authors of television serials today, playwrights devised endless variations on the same basic effects. So did Italian librettists: *Don Giovanni* was one among hundreds of comic operas. The difference was Mozart.

Serious opera, still an aristocratic genre, depended on virtuoso singers and made a class of its own; but in German-speaking lands comic opera, spoken plays, and other popular entertainments were not as distinct as they are for us. Plays often included songs and incidental music; Schikaneder put on open-air cavalry displays as well as *Hamlet*; the original singer of Pedrillo in *The Abduction from the Seraglio*, on the eve of the first night, played the lead in a made-over German version of *The School for Scandal*. Mozart himself devised and appeared in a harlequinade, and began to write two farces centred on the Viennese clown figure Hanswurst.

After the early Italian tours, he felt starved of theatre – not to mention opera. 'If only there were even a tolerably good theatre in Salzburg!' he wrote to his father once he had escaped to Vienna. This, like other strictures on his native town, was an exaggeration, but only in Vienna did he find theatres 'where all kinds of plays are *really well* performed'. Till then only the capital nearer at hand, Munich, gave him a chance to do what he most wanted – compose an opera.

He seems not to have minded what sort of opera he undertook. His letters at times express a preference for German or for Italian opera, for the comic or the serious genre. This seems to reflect the mood of the moment, the person he was writing to, or the opportunities that beckoned. His goal was opera: the kind mattered little – in Paris, aged twenty-two, he even proposed to take on the difficult local genre of *tragédie-lyrique*, spectacular opera with ballet – but as Italian opera dominated Europe outside France most of the works he eventually composed were to Italian librettos.

His Munich comic opera *La finta giardiniera* (The Pretended Garden Girl) (1775) had only three performances. Its score showed the mature style he had worked out at Salzburg in the previous couple of years, but he could not as yet match a profusion of fine music with control of the libretto and of the dramatic structure; too much of it is a sequence of arias, the characters' arbitrary ways repeat the clichés of dozens of comic operas, and it all goes on too long.

When the next invitation to Munich came, in the autumn of 1780, it was to write a serious opera, for a new court – that of the Elector Karl Theodor who, three years earlier at Mannheim, had failed to give Wolfgang a job. The Elector had taken with him to Munich the famed Mannheim orchestra and the Mannheim outlook on opera – strongly influenced, as was that of a few other courts, by Paris, in particular by the reform operas in which Gluck had sought to bring back the noble, grand simplicity contemporaries saw in the antique: a serious opera ought to work through declamation, powerful or brilliant choruses, impressive movement, and ballet as well as through the arias that were the Italian staple. The subject Mozart was given, *Idomeneo* – a non-biblical version of the story of Jephthah, who incautiously vowed to sacrifice the first being he met and then ran into his own child – came from a French *tragédie-lyrique* composed early in the century.

Though he did not say so in letters to his father – they tell us more about the making of this work than we know about any other – Mozart clearly jumped at the chance of writing something like the French opera he had missed in Paris: the words, by custom, would be Italian but the spirit would be mainly French. He had good singers and a fine orchestra and worked consciously at the height of his powers.

Idomeneo, long admired rather than performed, in recent years has come into its own as a sovereign work audiences want to hear.

Mozart quickly rode over the obstacle of having to use a libretto by the Salzburg court poet, the Abbé G. B. Varesco, that told the story clearly but was prolix; the third act was far too long at a time when, by custom, it ought to have been shorter than the others (third acts would soon drop out altogether). Varesco remained in Salzburg – everything had to be worked out through Leopold – and stood on his dignity, as a 'poet'-librettist was then entitled to do. Mozart answered his and his father's objections politely but made short work of them; these men of the previous generation had grown up with long recitatives and saw no need to change. Parts of the libretto, Wolfgang wrote, were too long and would have to be cut; if the librettist did not do it (retaining in the published libretto the words not set to music, a customary right) the composer would.

He made Varesco shorten the crucial speech by the voice of Neptune that lets Idomeneo off killing his son, and then himself shortened it again: 'if the speech of the Ghost in *Hamlet* were not so long, it would be far more effective' (wrong about the Ghost, in Shakespeare's own verse, but right in that he probably heard it as song, which moves more slowly; right too when he pointed out that in Varesco's draft Neptune's solemn oracle would have bored the audience). He 'had to be rude' to the noble supervisor of the opera house before he could get him to spend money on the trombones wanted to give Neptune an impressive backing; it took 'a desperate fight' (even then the trombones, it seems, failed to appear).

As in all eighteenth-century opera rehearsals, the composer was bound to accommodate, if he could, the singers who then mattered far more than he did. The men were the trouble. The two heroines – light and dark – were Dorothea and Elisabeth Wendling, sisters-in-law, both fine singers and old acquaintances from Mannheim days; with them all went smoothly. For the tenor Anton Raaff, then sixty-six, the title part was the last in a glorious career; affable but set in his ways, he need careful handling, and so did his voice. The second tenor,

Domenico Panzacchi, another veteran, was entitled to have his largely superfluous part built up. The castrato juvenile lead, Vincenzo Dal Prato, struck Mozart as 'rotten' and 'utterly useless'. Contrary to so dismissive a report, he had had fair experience and was musically 'learned'. Mozart's scorn probably came of Dal Prato's lack of expression: both he and Raaff 'spoil the recitative by singing it without any spirit or fire, and so monotonously. They are the most wretched actors that ever walked on a stage.' Mozart tried to put some 'spirit or fire' into them, but in the end cut down the highly dramatic recitative scene in which Idomeneo and his son-victim Idamante meet.

Panzacchi, in contrast, was a good actor: Mozart built up his plangent arioso, brooding on the fate of Crete ('Sventurata Sidon!'), but could not help writing two unnecessary arias to show off his coloratura. Raaff already had two arias but wanted a third: why not substitute one for the Act 3 quartet that gave him no chance to sing out? 'My very dear friend', Mozart replied, 'if I knew of one single note which ought to be altered in this quartet, I would alter it at once' (it was in fact the poignant climax of the work; when Mozart sang in it at home during his 1783 visit to Salzburg he broke down and left the room). Raaff acquiesced, the more easily because Mozart wrote him a third aria to sing at the very end of the opera, and had the words rewritten twice to suit him.

Such were the pains that went with the delivery of almost any opera; these happen to be unusually well documented. Nor was it out of the way for the first night to be put off (to 29 March 1781) or for everyone to realise, with some ten days to go, that the last act was far too long. The court would not want to lose a note of the final ballet – 'those confounded dances', Mozart called them; splendid, buoyant dances they are too. That meant cutting deep into the sung text.

Mozart had already decided that a duet for the intended sacrificial victim and his beloved (who wants to die in his stead) must be cut and the scene dispatched in recitative: the other characters would have to stand awkwardly about the sacrificial altar, 'and besides, the noble struggle between Idamante and Ilia would be too long and thus lose its whole force'. Now much more had to go: Panzacchi's second aria, Dal Prato's last aria, the beautiful last aria for Raaff that had caused so much trouble, even the magnificent aria of rage in which the dark heroine Elettra calls up the shades of Orestes and Ajax. Mozart had already pointed out the silliness of Varesco's clearing the stage at the denouement 'to allow Madame Elettra to be alone'. It was, all the same, just as uncomfortable for everyone to gawp while she raved at length. This cut may come of more than timekeeping; it may show the composer ruthlessly discarding musical splendour for the sake of dramatic impetus.

Idomeneo – this is the extraordinary thing – in the event achieved both. Its musical glories have never been in doubt. After witnessing about half the work in rehearsal the Elector said to Mozart 'Who would believe that such great things could be hidden in so small a head?' The musicians thought it 'wonderful' and 'strange'. The score surges at us on a wave of confident power. The great choruses of panic and plague still make the hair stand on end, just as the earlier barcarolle chorus wafts the most enticing sea-breeze. The solos and ensembles for the chief characters fit them and are nearly all memorable – but for Idamante's arias, a sign, perhaps, that Mozart had little trust in Dal Prato. Declamatory passages – the high priest's appeal to Idomeneo to obey the god and save the people, among several – achieve high eloquence.

One cause is the apt invention that wells up unendingly beneath them in the orchestra. No other Mozart opera so revels in what each instrument can do, as well as in chromaticism and other means of heightened expression, without overbearing the voices or going on too long. To secure momentum, the musical action keeps on at the end of the overture and of several numbers, without a halt for applause. The wonderful quartet Raaff objected to – 'Andrò ramingo e solo' – ends without a cadence after taking the harrowed chief characters through remote keys and areas of feeling. The work is a musician's delight.

Idomeneo remains an expansive court opera whose story has to be fed a monster, a plague, and the oddity of Electra as the other woman if it is not to run out too soon. It will never be as popular as *Figaro*. It is, all the same, the composer's masterpiece, in the old guild sense of the work a young craftsman produced to show his mastery. No wonder that in Vienna Mozart longed to play it to the emperor, did play it to the noble superintendent of opera and other connoisseurs, tried to have an adapted version put on, and finally, in 1786, revised it for performance by noble amateurs, with Idamante no longer a castrato but a tenor.

The original 1781 production showed that Mozart now understood the needs of sung drama – from the avoidance of too many stressed notes on the vowel 'i' to the awkwardness of asides when they must be repeated on musical grounds: he would not have them. He got the movement over the long span right – rarest of achievements – even though he had to make cuts; the rightness is inward and performances of varyingly cut texts can all work in the theatre, while a concert performance of nearly all Mozart wrote makes a cornucopia. Furthermore, Mozart discovered that he could, in Charles Rosen's words, make the music 'not so much an expression of the text' as 'an equivalent for the dramatic action' – a revolutionary achievement: 'for the first time on the operatic stage, the music could follow the dramatic action while still arriving at form that could justify itself . . . on purely internal grounds'.[1]

This is probably close to what Mozart had in mind when he wrote in October 1781, about seven months after the first night, 'in an opera the poetry must be altogether the obedient daughter of the music'. He was by then working on *The Abduction from the Seraglio*, acknowledged that Gottlieb Stephanie's libretto was no great shakes as verse, but approved of words 'written solely for the music and not shoved in here and there to suit some miserable rhyme'; the ideal would be attained 'when a good composer, who understands the stage, and is talented enough to make sound suggestions, meets an able poet . . .' That would happen only when Mozart and Lorenzo Da Ponte came together in 1786 to write *Figaro*.

Meanwhile *Seraglio* was not his first try at establishing himself in

Vienna as an opera composer. The emperor since 1776 had chosen to back 'national' German opera or Singspiel – comic opera with spoken dialogue – a venture that was to expire in 1783 for lack of good material. In 1780, before the invitation came to write *Idomeneo*, Mozart wrote but left unfinished and untitled part of a Singspiel now known as *Zaide*. It put to work the enthusiasm he had picked up the year before, on the way back from Paris, for 'melodrama' (music accompanying speech). The notable thing about it is not the melodramas – though one at least is eloquent – but the quantity of fine theatre music Mozart was prepared to leave on the shelf, without reusing any of it in later works. Like the cuts in *Idomeneo*, this speaks for the wealth of invention he could draw on and royally let go to waste.

His reason for dropping *Zaide* was no doubt that *Seraglio* then came up: it told almost the same story. Turkish subjects were popular, and so was 'Turkish' music, noisy with triangle and drum. Vienna had barely escaped Turkish conquest in 1683; wars recurred through the eighteenth century, and would again in 1788. A tale of Europeans captured by Turks made for a pleasurable shudder at thoughts of rape in the harem or summary execution by bowstring, and then for joy at escape from tyranny. Islam was represented as both farcical and cruel. At most Stephanie, adapting an earlier libretto, made the Pasha relent at the close and so outdo Christians in 'enlightened' magnanimity.

By late July 1781 Mozart had been commissioned to undertake the work. To begin with he wrote fast; for accidental reasons, however, the original September deadline receded again and again and the first night came only on 16 July 1782. He therefore had plenty of time – not an unmixed blessing. *Seraglio* laid an excess of fine music over a modest, somewhat rickety dramatic structure – 'too many notes', as the emperor perhaps said. In German-speaking countries it was an immediate and lasting success (not that this brought the composer any more money; when he tried to make some with a vocal score, a pirate publication forestalled him). Elsewhere *Seraglio* has always lagged a shade behind the three great Italian comedies and *The Magic Flute*.

Spoken dialogue (rather wooden) meant lost opportunities for ensemble; the regular beat of the German verse made the musical expression of feeling at times a little four-square. Mozart was in part responsible for changes to the libretto that blew up a slight work but still did not get it to hang together properly.

He made Stephanie provide new words, at least once to music he had already composed. It was almost certainly he who demanded a lavish quartet as the new Act 2 finale; the quartet, marvellous in itself, put in the shade the climax of the story in Act 3 – the failed abduction itself, now reduced to speech. He also put in a vast display aria for the heroine ('Martern aller Arten') right on top of her moving aria of despair ('Traurigkeit'), and introduced it with a sixty-bar ritornello during which she and her captor (who has just threatened her with torture) have to stand glaring at one another – unless, as in some modern stagings, they deflate the tension with irrelevant byplay.

One cause was the usual need to please the singers: here, to 'sacrifice', in Mozart's words, 'a little to the flexible throat of Mlle Cavalieri' – the coloratura specialist who sang the heroine – as he had already done in her first aria 'Ach, ich liebte'. He admired the tenor Valentin Adamberger and wrote him three arias; the latter two seem accomplished but a trifle abstract after the lively sentiment of the first, 'O wie ängstlich', with its delightful 'heartbeat' underlay for violins in octaves, gentle high note, sudden modulations at pangs of distress, and woodwind-charged accompaniments that recur in the minor, all within minutes of curtain-up. A more fundamental reason for his writing 'too many notes' in 'Martern aller Arten' and elsewhere was sheer delight in the orchestra: 'Martern', like Ilia's 'Se il padre perdei' in *Idomeneo*, is a concerto for the voice and four instruments, but the earlier aria – not on so large a scale – is better proportioned to the work as a whole. In *Seraglio* music-making at times got out of hand.

Where Mozart's exuberance did nothing but good was in the part of the boorish overseer Osmin. The bass Ludwig Fischer had a wide range and acting ability which the composer exploited to the full in bubbling arias of triumph and rage. That Mozart spread himself in

Osmin's part helped the work: it brightened the farcical side, gave it a dangerous edge, and, as the music was properly fast, kept up the necessary speed or even restored it when other numbers had let it go. In telling his father about the aria 'Solche hergelaufne Laffen' Mozart set out his operatic creed:

> as Osmin's rage gradually increases, there comes (just when the aria seems to be at an end) the allegro assai, which is in a totally different metre and in a different key; this is bound to be very effective. For just as a man in such a towering rage oversteps all the bounds of order, moderation, and propriety and completely forgets himself, so must the music too forget itself. But since passions . . . must never be expressed to the point of exciting disgust, and as music, even in the most terrible situations, must never offend the ear, but must please the listener, or in other words must never cease to be music, I have not chosen a key foreign to F (in which the aria is written) but one related to it – not the nearest, D minor, but the more remote A minor.

Seraglio could and can be enjoyed as a string of delightful numbers – not only those named, but also the final duet for the seemingly doomed lovers. This is earnest, at first tragic. It bears out another of Mozart's ideas, stated a couple of years later when he was working on another operatic project: according to the libretto one character was to sing words 'very disconsolate and despairing' to a melody which another would echo to words 'most comforting and hopeful'. This, Mozart wrote, was dramatically 'out of the question' and was anyhow out of date (which would not prevent Rossini, forty years later, from still making two characters voice divergent feelings to the same tune; as a dramatist in music Mozart was a pioneer). In the *Seraglio* duet the lovers sing different melodies as they compete in self-sacrifice – here, almost, is the duet Mozart left out of *Idomeneo* – but together when they join in facing their doom. Still 'too many notes' just ahead of the denouement? Perhaps, but what notes!

After *Seraglio* Mozart went on looking for openings. By 1783 Joseph II had gone back to patronising Italian comic opera. One project Mozart started on was *L'oca del Cairo* (*The Cairo Goose*), to a text by

Varesco. He now had a short way with librettists: if the opera was to succeed Varesco 'must alter or recast the libretto as much and as often as I wish'. He composed much of the first act but gave up, probably because 'this goose story' was too inane even for Italian comic opera. He started on another, not much more promising text, *Lo sposo deluso* (*The Disappointed Bridegroom*), but composed even less. Both fragments contain fine pieces – never reused – alongside routine ones. With an excellent Italian comic opera troupe installed in the Burgtheater, headed by the Anglo-Italian soprano Nancy Storace and the comic bass Francesco Benucci, it seemed Mozart would get no chance. At most he was allowed to write extra numbers for operas by Italian composers.

Early in 1786 he got to compose a one-act German squib, again by Stephanie, *Der Schauspieldirektor* (*The Impresario*), to share the bill in a performance at court with an Italian libretto set by Salieri. Both dealt with rivalries among opera artists, a subject rehashed for most of the century, but Salieri had much the better text (it would one day inspire Richard Strauss's *Capriccio*). All Mozart could get out of his was a sparkling overture, two mock-display arias, and a brisk little trio.

His big chance, though, was at hand. In October 1785 he had started work on *The Marriage of Figaro*; by November he was 'up to the eyes' in it. About the rehearsal period we know little. The Irish tenor Michael Kelly, who sang minor parts in the first performance, recorded that at the dress rehearsal Benucci's stentorian rendering of Figaro's mock-military aria 'Non più andrai' had all the singers and players calling out 'Bravo! Bravo! Maestro, viva, viva, grande Mozart', the players beating with their bows on their stands. 'The little man [in his crimson pelisse and gold-laced cocked hat] acknowledged, by repeated obeisances, his thanks.' The first night on 1 May 1786 was a success, perhaps with a minority. The work none the less entered the repertory throughout Europe; there it stayed – the first opera, in Charles Rosen's words, 'that [has] never had to be revived'. Some think it the greatest ever written.

Though critics to begin with objected, as usual, that it was all too complex and you could not hum the tunes, one, Bernhard Anselm Weber (unrelated to Constanze or to the later composer), was to pick out in 1789 what are now generally seen as *Figaro*'s outstanding merits:

> great and beautiful, full of new ideas and unexpected turns, full of art, fire, and genius. Now we are enchanted by beautiful, charming song; now we are made to smile at subtle, comic wit and fancy; now we admire the naturally conceived and superbly executed planning . . . Mozart . . . ventures on impetuous and fiery sallies, and how bold are his harmonies! . . . he shows that he possesses a true talent for the comic-dramatic style . . .

The arias, many of them beautiful – Weber wrote – fitted the characters; the two trios in Acts 1 and 2 were 'full of art and expression'; the letter duet for the women, with oboe and bassoon obbligato, was 'nature itself'. Above all, the long finale of Act 2 was 'the masterpiece of the whole opera . . . full of wit, and originally and truly depicted'. Only the Act 3 sextet that follows the disclosure of Figaro's parentage – a glorious number, joyfully ludicrous, then intimately ecstatic – somewhat baffled Weber, perhaps because it was not well sung in the performance he was reviewing.

With his remark on 'the comic-dramatic style' Weber implied that the music had become 'the equivalent of the dramatic action' or, one might say, *was* the dramatic action. The achievement was Mozart's, but also Da Ponte's, with a nudge from Paisiello's *The Barber of Seville* and *King Theodore in Venice*, both given in Vienna in the previous three years. These works had shown how a fizzing stage comedy and a clever satire could each be made into an opera worth experiencing as a dramatic and musical whole. Da Ponte went further and built a stage action at once solid and fleet. Mozart's share in the libretto is undocumented; his masterly handling of its structure as music drama suggests that he had a share, and he clearly thought up one device both funny and insightful – Susanna's repeated attempts to say 'yes' to the count's urgings, which come out as 'no' (Freud was to mention it in his essay on slips of the tongue as evidence of the unconscious).

The twenty-minute finale of Act 2, picked out by Weber, remains the great example of music as dramatic action. A chain of ensembles, held together by slyly recurrent phrases that work their way round the singers and orchestra, matches every turn in the plot and gradually screws down the tension. Italian composers had for some years worked up such linked finales, where all the singers came together in mounting confusion, but none ever achieved one so masterly and so exhilarating. Almost throughout the opera, proportions and timing are right. The only flaw, an overlong string of arias in the last act, can be remedied by dropping the unnecessary arias for Marcellina and Basilio: Mozart clearly put them in because the singers of these minor parts were entitled to one each.

Two months before the fall of the Bastille it would not have been prudent for Weber to say that *Figaro* was revolutionary. Explicit political critique was never on. Did the work implicitly attack at its foundations the old regime now about to collapse? Scholars disagree. Left-wing, particularly Marxist writers tend to say yes, others no.

Comic opera had its own class structure: 'serious', usually upperclass parts had more elaborate music, 'comic', often plebeian parts had simpler music. In *Figaro*, Michael Robinson has pointed out, the music for the count and countess is apt for 'serious' parts, but that for the servants Figaro, Susanna, and Marcellina becomes more serious as the opera goes on, with Susanna's accompanied recitative and aria 'Giunse alfin il momento / Deh vieni, non tardar' the paradisal centre of the last act: 'the lower classes are rising to the (musical) level of their superiors'. Later in the act, she and Figaro (and their music) mock those superiors' grand manner.

Nearer the bone, Figaro's Act 1 aria 'Se vuol ballare' tackles (though in his absence) the noble employer who means to cuckold him. It is a minuet, an upper-class dance – here, a lightly hammering, aggressive one. The count may wish to dance; Figaro will 'play the tune' – a clear threat to take control, perhaps of more than the situation at hand. In general, the humanity of all the characters lifts the work out of the mechanical role distribution of comic opera; only the small part of the stuttering, venal judge is a cartoon.

An attack on sexual oppression by alleged superiors – noblemen, perhaps men in general – could be more open than any political critique. Beaumarchais's play turned on it. Two delightful women, sexually betrayed or threatened by the same man, take the initiative; at least as much as Figaro, they bring about the count's discomfiture and – perhaps fleeting – repentance. Da Ponte kept the theme intact. The words of Figaro's aria against women – with the mocking horns Mozart put in – are conventional, but they arise out of his having misunderstood the women's tactics; when he understands, he joins in.

Mozart exploited this theme of sexual threat and retort in music that, like his Vienna piano concertos, delicately, boldly ranges over the possibilities of the erotic. Da Ponte's Italian words helped: neat and playful. *Figaro* is more erotic in tone than the opera supposed to be erotic by definition, *Don Giovanni*.

Sexual awareness permeates the noble household, embodied in the page Cherubino with his search for a woman, any woman, to whom he can offer his chaotic impulses. His aria 'Non so più cosa son, cosa faccio' is perhaps the first, certainly the most complete expression in music of adolescent sexuality, Susanna's 'Deh vieni, non tardar' the most enchanting invitation from a woman to a man – with the extra spice of being addressed seemingly to the wrong man, for the right man to overhear. The ambiguities of the scene in which she and the countess dress Cherubino as a girl – now as a rule coarsened by producers – likewise balance emotion and pleasantry. So caressing a moment as the letter duet lifts pleasure to a height of beauty at its apparent simplest – what Weber, an early German Romantic, probably meant by 'nature itself'. The countess who joins in that duet can, in 'Dove sono', be heard moving from regret for lost joys to a determination to win back; her music distils a femininity easily hurt, yet insightful and open-hearted.

Music does it; the words are apt, but they only set going the flow of music insinuating (the many varied wind accompaniments), thrustful (the count's aria), pathetic (Barbarina's tiny aria as she searches for the lost pin). At the end the count refuses to forgive anybody; the countess emerges, confounds him; he in turn begs forgiveness; her answer on the printed page is almost throwaway: 'I am more pliable than you, I say yes.' Mozart made it into a slow arching phrase for which Shakespeare's words about mercy ('it droppeth down from heaven upon the place beneath') are right. The stageful of people in the night garden repeat it; their voices twice soar up in grave joy, recede; the orchestra traverses the hush in a downward phrase. Humanity collected is rapt in a shaft of grace; the moment seems to expand, it casts, both on the emotional whirl that has gone before and on the concluding burst of joy it sets off, a light from the garden of Eden.

This sense of the unearthly glimpsed from a world of human wilfulness and complex feeling is the mark of *Don Giovanni*, Mozart's next opera. He wrote it because *Figaro* had triumphed in Prague, another Habsburg capital (of the kingdom of Bohemia). When he travelled there by invitation in January 1787, together with Constanze and his friend the clarinettist Anton Stadler, his Vienna career as a pianist-composer who lived by playing his own concertos was over. Prague, then as now, was soaked in music; it specially valued Mozart's. *Figaro* had just been put on, to huge acclaim. 'Nothing here', Mozart found, 'is talked of, played, hummed, sung, or whistled except for *Figaro*.' The impresario of the mainly young opera troupe gave him a contract for another opera; this, first performed on 29 October 1787 to another libretto by Lorenzo Da Ponte, was *Don Giovanni*.

Wolfgang and Constanze again made the journey to Prague for the three-week rehearsal period. They stayed part of the time with their friends Franz Xaver and Josepha Duschek (Dušek), composer and singer, on the castle hill overlooking the city, and were made much of; Da Ponte joined them for a week. Mozart knew the company and the lovely, intimate Nostitz Theatre (still in use); he had most of the music ready, though he composed the second finale on the spot – the overture too, in a hurry just before the dress rehearsal.

That overture told the audience of the extraordinary work it was about to hear. Grim chords and rushing scales speak of a visitant from another world (they recur when the Commander's statue visits Don Giovanni in the finale); the rest is comedy.

By 1787 the centuries-old Don Juan archetype worked on those two levels. The tale of the 'stone guest' – the outraged father who haunts his daughter's seducer, his own murderer – had dwindled into a puppet show; a recent libretto which Da Ponte quarried took it as a joke. Molière's play of 1665, however, had brought in a philosophical theme. His Juan was a libertine as the seventeenth century understood the term: not just a sexual predator but a materialist who set out to question, even to challenge revealed Christian doctrine. When, in the opera, Giovanni leads his guests in the chorus 'Viva la libertà', 'libertà' means chiefly the unaccustomed freedom of a socially mixed, semi-public ball, with a few of the dancers masked – a kind many of the original audience had taken part in – but it may hint at libertinism in this sense. What it does not hint at – only after the French Revolution could anyone suppose it did – is political liberty.

The Romantic nineteenth century misunderstood a good deal else about the work. Already by 1789, for advanced German writers, the music was noble but tied to a demeaning libretto (the hidebound complained as usual that it was over-complex and lacked 'heart'). The Danish philosopher Søren Kierkegaard, in an 1843 essay, saw Don Giovanni as an abstract embodiment of desire, who pursued through all his adventures an ideal of womanhood. Already in 1810 the German Romantic author E. T. A. Hoffmann fancied that Giovanni's quarry Donna Anna was in love with him, had indeed been seduced by him, and – still bewitched at curtain-fall – put off her fiancé Don Ottavio with an excuse. Nowadays many productions have Giovanni, with Anna in pursuit, stumble on hitching up his trousers; one at least has shown the rape. All this comes of misunderstanding words and music. The Romantics needed to make a supposedly trivial story worthy of Mozart; obsession with literal sexuality has now brought back some of their fancies.[2]

A further problem is that, when Mozart in 1788 adapted the work to suit Viennese taste and the singers available, he put in a replacement

13 The graveyard scene in *Don Giovanni*, designed by Joseph Quaglio for a production at Mannheim in 1789

aria for Ottavio ('Dalla sua pace'), a new farcical duet for the lower-class characters Leporello and Zerlina, and a big new aria ('Mi tradì') for Elvira, now raised from 'seconda donna' to 'prima' alongside Anna; the last was another 'sacrifice to the flexible throat of Mlle Cavalieri'. Either the Prague or the Vienna version, one can argue, works in the theatre. Opera managements, however, as a rule put in both Ottavio's new aria and the one it replaced ('Il mio tesoro', just as fine), while they leave in 'Mi tradì' but not the farcical scene that balanced it. We scarcely ever hear what Mozart intended; what we do hear is more lumbering than it should be.

Mozart's is a comic opera shot through with intimations of another world. That it is a comic opera, at times conventional, is beyond doubt. Leporello's record of his master's conquests follows on several catalogue arias in works of the previous few years; Mozart so dramatised it in music that it is the only one remembered. He did much more. In the last scene a blast of supernatural power sweeps over the earth, where, even then, cowardly Leporello mutters his all-too-human fright; it breaks the comic opera mould, but once Don Giovanni has vanished the other characters put it together again and restore the human norm. Again, music does it: 'the mysteries of harmony, tremendous and beautiful', in Julian Rushton's words, 'are Mozart's response to the tragic and supernatural elements' in the story; the Commander's modulation from D to A minor on 'Non si pasce' 'seems to traverse the tonal universe'. Da Ponte played down the moral and religious element; Mozart put it back in.

Yet the work is comic – not just in form but in its view of life. Giovanni is not a forerunner of the Byronic hero, glamorous and self-pitying. He is, Bernard Williams has pointed out, the negative centre of the opera – the black hole the other characters may be sucked into. This is shown by his having no aria other than one short burst of fire-works and one merely functional; those (and the serenade) apart, he is all musical interplay with the rest. 'Fin ch'han dal vino' with its ribald bassoon octave speaks Giovanni's all-purpose, directionless energy. He exploits his society, at times brutally, but does not belong to it; he is 'a brigand in his own country'. Comedy expels him to bring back a world of relationships.

The three women Mozart surrounds him with look to make up Everywoman. Donna Anna's musical utterance is all lyrical or heroic, often in noble, arc-like melodic shapes. The man she loves, Ottavio, is not the wimp sometime shown; he does the right and tender thing, as his arias declare, likewise his part in the tremendous oath duet after the Commander's death. Donna Elvira, bamboozled into a fake marriage, then abandoned, sings much of the time in angular, antique style. Hers was originally a 'mezzo carattere' – half-comic – part, taken by a second-rank artist; Mozart seems to have thought – as would most of his con-temporaries – that her hungry, abject love for her seducer was funny as well as pathetic. Neither of these women has much to do with Eros in his everyday undress. When they and Ottavio join in the trio 'Protegga il giusto cielo', we indeed glimpse a justice 'enskied and sainted'.

The third woman, the peasant Zerlina, closer to earth, is easily drawn to a rich nobleman, though she pulls back at the last moment. Eros informs her music, as well as some of the ensembles, in particular those where Giovanni looks like succeeding. Elvira forsakes her angularity to join in 'Ah taci, ingiusto core', the balcony trio that opens the serious business of Act 2: Giovanni's voice in the dark seduces her all over again to come down and throw herself away on his disguised servant. The crucial part of the trio runs in mellifluous, insinuating waves above an accompaniment as beautiful as Mozart knew how to make it, Elvira's voice recurring to an ecstatic high note: at once sublime and appallingly comic.

Wave-like or stepwise melodies – varied and sharply characterised – all but let Giovanni seduce Zerlina as well. Because he talks down to her youth and naivety the duet 'Là ci darem la mano', and the later praise of her hands that feel like junket and smell like roses, sound innocent. Knowing innocence rules Zerlina's own seduction of her estranged fiancé Masetto ('Batti, batti'), while the solace she brings him after Giovanni has beaten him up ('Vedrai, carino') distils sexual charm at its lightest; 'heartbeat' music finds literal warrant as Zerlina discloses her secret remedy by placing her fiancé's hand on her breast.

The control of structure shown in *Figaro* is again at work – not quite so smooth. Whatever the version used, the first half of Act 2 loses headway, in part because Mozart spreads himself in the sextet: the characters have to keep up an ensemble of perplexity for seven or eight minutes, a problem dramatically when most repetitions for musical ends come *after* they find out that 'Giovanni' is Leporello in disguise. The change to a remote major key that signals the discovery is astonishing and the whole piece a musical wonder, but earlier ensembles – the Act 1 quartet with Elvira and Giovanni each trying to win over Anna and Ottavio, for instance – achieve a fitter pace. So does the big Act 1 finale with its famous layering of three dance orchestras: producers who come up with something for Giovanni to do at the end (swing on a chandelier, jump out of the window etc.) do not realise that at such first-half curtains nothing was meant to happen other than everyone confronting each other to fast music. Audiences did not worry about how the characters got away to sing again in Act 2.

An opera that can indulge, just ahead of the statue's terrific entrance, in a joke about a servant pinching a mouthful of his master's roast pheasant (not incidental but fully exploited in the music), punctuates other scenes with glimpses of the uncanny. When, at the sword-thrust that kills the Commander, three low men's voices plunge into grave, brief discourse; when, in the cemetery, two of them fall abashed at the statue's unlooked-for 'yes'; when Giovanni serenades Elvira and we are held astonished between incipient tears and laughter, Mozart lets us glimpse the Other – an Other the anti-hero cannot acknowledge.

The Other glimmers in and out of *Così fan tutte* as well, but with light, near-invisible step. This was the last of Mozart's and Da Ponte's Italian operas. Commissioned in late 1789, a time when Mozart was writing very little, it signalled the end of his major phase as composer, while its appearance a few months into the French Revolution showed it balanced on the cusp of change.

Little is reliably known of its preparation. Mozart, it is clear, demanded changes to the libretto (which Salieri had given up after composing two numbers). As he went along he made one hurried cut that left a musical loose end; he also dropped a big aria for Guglielmo, the earthier of the two lovers, in favour of a lighter one, and appears to have cut out in performance Ferrando's 'Ah, lo veggio', an aria too long and elaborate for the scene it was in. Twice, in December and again in January, he invited Haydn to a rehearsal together with his own friend and creditor Michael Puchberg. The first-night audience on 26 January 1790, it seems, welcomed *Così fan tutte* – as a routine comic opera; after that year's run of performances, interrupted by Joseph II's death, Vienna did not hear the work again in its original form until 1850.

Its tale of two couples' erotic feigning and betrayal set up, in 1790, resonances we may miss. The cult of sensibility – the ego rapt with its own choice feelings – had been going for much of the century; in the past decade or more, the sorrows of Goethe's Werther had provoked a few actual and many more imaginary suicides. All this is in the work, first in the many calls the two pairs of lovers make on death to end their woes or their disgrace – the sword-thrusts proffered or clamoured for, the fake poisonings – but also in an onrush of genuine passion at the absurdest moments, as when Fiordiligi surrenders to the new lover, still wearing bits of the uniform meant for the battlefield where she was to seek out the old one.

Like war in Jane Austen, the news from revolutionary Paris that circulated among the audience is in the work – between the lines. It echoes *Figaro* and other comic operas of the 1780s in giving voice to the tide of discontent with privilege and hierarchy. The maid Despina's scorn for her 'betters' is a new-minted cliché within the convention of the venal, cynical maid: the lower orders have grown routinely insolent.

What we share, if not with the 1790 audience then with slightly later ones, is a problem with the story. *Così fan tutte* has dated twice, the second time in our own day.

The later Romantics shushed it out of the canon. In an earnest age, the work sullied Woman, mocked Love, and demeaned its maker – unless, like Wagner, you opined that Mozart, faced with such poor stuff, showed his greatness by turning out a mediocre score. As early as 1791 the poet-dramatist F. L. Schröder called the libretto 'a miserable thing, which lowers all women'; hearing the music in the theatre failed to change his mind. The trouble was the seeming outrage on female 'delicacy'. *Così fan tutte* all but fell out of the repertory.

It came back after 1910, with the movement for a 'return to order' and to coolness in all the arts. Producers at times overcooled it, turning its characters into puppets and setting it in unhistorical 'Dresden china' wigs and panniers (it belongs to the early neo-classical age of Lady Hamilton; its heroines would dress in muslin simplicity, their furniture take after rediscovered Pompeii).

Then, in our own day, came the new feminism. *Così fan tutte* was dubious all over again, not now because it questioned women's delicacy but because it showed them manipulated by men – who got away with it. How intolerably trivial that, after having been brought to declare themselves to new lovers, Fiordiligi and Dorabella should go back to the original fiancés who had undone them – two sets of betrayers betrayed, spliced at the drop of a final chorus. Some thought Mozart, deeply in sympathy with the women, in his music had subverted the conventions of his age. Ours has set its own convention that in the theatre the original ending is out: instead of forgetting the previous twelve hours, the new pairs stay sullenly together, or they unscramble but remain thoroughly put out, or they all go off shamed and angered, determined, it seems, never to marry, or (hey presto!) the women at the last moment fob off the men with substitutes. The manipulators Don Alfonso and Despina may also be shown penitent or resentful, in flat contradiction to the lines they sing.

What did Mozart intend in *Così fan tutte?* Any opera is bound to be recreated through the minds of those who hear it. We do, all the same, need to put that question if we are not to read into the work meanings it is incapable of bearing.

The plot was highly conventional. Modern scholars have shown that it goes back through two threads – to a fourteenth-century tale of a man who bets on a woman's virtue, and to another, launched in antiquity and current in much eighteenth-century theatre both spoken and sung, of disguise, sometimes double disguise, as a means to winning one's own beloved. The audience were familiar with these clichés from long theatregoing experience, probably a good deal more than from the classic Latin and Italian authors Da Ponte alluded to. That experience also yielded a conventional social framework for the opera, namely opera itself.

To its first audience *Così fan tutte* was, as Daniel Heartz has written, 'an opera about opera'. Its symmetries were the stuff of opera and opera companies: leading singers not just evenly matched but taking over each other's musical line, as the men do in their early trios with Don Alfonso and the women in their opening duet – a hint that both pairs will prove interchangeable. When their lovers have supposedly gone off to the wars, the women parody serious opera in Dorabella's aria of rage, 'Smanie implacabili' – a take-off of Elettra's ravings in

Idomeneo – and in Fiordiligi's 'Come scoglio', not just a parody of the words and music current in arias of defiance but a guying by the original singer of her own heroic manner, which exploited her uncommon range by spanning vocal peaks and troughs. *Così fan tutte* is in a long Italian tradition of theatre playing at and with theatre.

We may even imagine the original audience (and Mozart) identifying the two heroines as opera singers. What other young women of means would have come to Naples without a visible protector? Are they not opera singers between engagements, who have formed engagements of another sort with young officers met on the way? Eighteenth-century plays and librettos abounded in such pairs of singers (in plays they might be actresses), because under despotic regimes the eccentricities of theatre people were among the few safe subjects, because in a hugely sexist society performers were among the few women able to love as they chose while keeping some respectability, and because operas and plays of that date had at least two leading women's parts.

We need not strain to understand how a nobleman could write in his diary after the first performance that the music was 'charming' and the story 'rather amusing'. *Così fan tutte* was a happy variation on a known theme; it diffused happiness, a feeling prized by eighteenth-century people, today often lost sight of or thought blameworthy.

That apart, it was serious only in its fingertip didacticism. The original title, *The School for Lovers*, and the last lines show what that meant: 'lovers, don't strike attitudes, make allowances for human frailty, be reasonable'. To us that sounds civilised, yet the work, like the manipulative Don Alfonso, keeps a strain of 'enlightened' ruthlessness, at once harsher and tenderer than we can bear (because harsh while tender, and unconcerned to explain).

In the quintet of farewell what goes on is deceptive farce; the music points it up in the women's exaggerated, broken diction, interspersed with violin sobs, as well as in less obvious jokes (Fiordiligi abandoning her long-held high note just as she sings the word 'constant'). Yet all along Mozart pours out blessing in what Bruce Alan Brown has called 'luminous texture and harmonies, which coexist with the comic elements without in any way interferring with them': the pizzicato bass accompaniment 'seems to hold off indefinitely the moment of departure';

> the lovers leave off their fragmentary utterances and soar in new harmonic directions . . . the viola line is freed from its previous oscillations, and moves in gentle counterpoint with the voices, as a wordless, sympathetic observer. As the women respond to the men's farewell, a crescendo, the splitting of the viola line, and a deceptive cadence combine to suggest a sudden welling-up of emotion.

Yet Don Alfonso has kept up almost throughout his sotto voce comment 'If I don't laugh I shall burst': we are to weep with and laugh at Fiordiligi and Dorabella, because their emotion is true and false, all at once. In the subsequent trio ('Soave sia il vento'), wishing the departing lovers a fair wind and a gentle passage, Alfonso opens his pursed lips to join the women in a breath of loveliness, its poignancy touched in by the aching modulation on 'desir'.

So it goes: at moments of truest pathos, when Fiordiligi in her soliloquy aria 'Per pietà' pleads for her 'absent' lover's understanding, Mozart sets the horns tootling their signal of cuckoldry, unmistakable as they were in Figaro's diatribe – and the horns are his idea, not Da Ponte's. Yet Fiordiligi's music also suggests that she, like Ferrando, has it in her to join in the duet of overmastering love they eventually fall into ('Fra gli amplessi'); Ferrando too, from having set out to manipulate her in revenge, all at once finds that his emotion is real. Even Dorabella, so readily faithless, shows in the charm of her aria about love the little thief ('E' amor un ladroncello') that this faithless one is lovable enough to dispel all reservations.

Thanks to music, seduction is not just a manoeuvre; it is in the air. The serenade that opens the garden scene, like many other passages in *Così fan tutte*, shows Mozart's orchestration at its ravishing height, at once limpid and charged with sonorities undreamt of; almost anyone would yield to it. Near the end, as the two new couples, about to sign the marriage contract, toast their future and prepare to forget the past ('E nel tuo, nel mio bicchiero'), Mozart unfolds a canon quartet of serene inward beauty – or it would be a canon quartet if Guglielmo in an aside (the musical line lies too high for him) did not go his own way, muttering imprecations. The two pairs have just heard the chorus wish them the burlesque fertility of chickens, they will soon plunge into exposure and mock threats of bloodshed, but for a couple of minutes something holds them – a celestial otherness.

Così fan tutte stands at the crossroads of the trivial and the heavenly: the people so trivial, the music so much what the philosopher and theologian Simone Weil, in one of her last notebooks, called beauty – 'the real presence of God', 'experimental proof of the possibility of Incarnation'. She also wrote that to love human beings as God does is to love them 'for the nonentities they are'. Mozart is the theologian's composer because he shares something of the divine objectivity. Nowhere is this truer than in Così fan tutte, a comedy that sends up humankind and itself.

5 Mozart and God

Mozart's innermost feelings about life, death, and the universe are to be found not in his church music but here and there in his secular works: so we now tend to think. We may be wrong.

Since the French Revolution and the Romantic movement – that is, since shortly before Mozart's death – Christian faith has, among educated Europeans, been problematic. By many dismissed or ridiculed, it has, for those who still hold to it, become an earnest, even tormented experience. 'If God does not exist, everything is permitted': the thought that obsesses Ivan Karamazov in Dostoevsky's novel emerged when, for intellectuals like Ivan, God indeed looked like disappearing. Faith must come to terms with the dread of emptiness and the persistence of evil, or take to irrational enthusiasm.

In the eighteenth century, men and women could still hold without question to straightforward Christian belief and be cheerful about it. The Emperor Joseph II thought monks and nuns in enclosed orders who gave themselves over to contemplative prayer were wasting their own and society's resources: clergy should work in the parishes, help the needy, guide the people in right living, and educate the young. That did not make Joseph other than a sincere Catholic. His faith, like that of many contemporaries, was intent on doing good in this world; it may have opened the way to a generalised theism, or to an ethic that would do without God altogether, but he did not himself question a supernatural reality or the account of it given by Christian doctrine. Such faith could be equable.

So could Mozart's, as he stated it. What he had to say comes mostly in letters to his parents, and may show him on best behaviour. 'God's will is always best': this comment on the expected death of a family friend, addressed to his mother when he was fourteen, sums it up. He said it again eight years later in 1778 when his mother died in Paris, adding, to his father and sister: 'we shall see her again ... we shall live together far more happily and blissfully than ever in this world ... When God wills it, I am ready.' As the danger to his mother's life became clear – Wolfgang had already written to a close Salzburg friend who was to break the news to Leopold – he had prayed 'for two things only – a happy death for her, and strength and courage for myself; and God in his goodness heard my prayer...'

Mozart needed that strength and courage in April 1787 when he learned that his father in turn was seriously ill (he died just over six weeks later, on 28 May). To Leopold he wrote that he was used to preparing for the worst; the parenthesis 'you know what I mean' may hint at Masonic teaching, but it could just as well, or better, refer to the experience he had gone through in Paris at the time of his mother's death:

> As death, when we consider it closely, is the true goal of our existence, I have formed during the last few years such close relations with this best and truest friend of mankind that his image is not only no longer terrifying to me, but is indeed very soothing and consoling! And I thank my God for graciously granting me the opportunity (you know what I mean) of learning that death is the key which unlocks the door to our true happiness. I never lie down at night without reflecting that – young as I am – I may not live to see another day. Yet no one of all my acquaintances could say that in company I am morose or disgruntled.

Much of this came from a contemporary philosophical work. In quarrying it Wolfgang was most likely sincere: people often need books to speak their feelings for them.

Not that we need depend on what Mozart told his family. The sincerity of his Christian faith shows plainly in words he wrote for himself alone. Three months or so after Leopold, Sigmund Barisani died – Wolfgang's Salzburg contemporary, close friend, and doctor. Under Barisani's entry in his album Mozart recorded the loss of this 'dearest, best of friends': 'He is at rest! – but I, we, all that knew him well – we shall *never* be at rest again – until we have the felicity of seeing him again – in a better world – and *never more to part.*'

Death provokes such statements. Like most eighteenth-century men and women, Wolfgang was expert in it. Though only thirty when he wrote his farewell to Barisani, he had heard of the deaths of friends, relatives, colleagues, his own children as often as most of us do in our sixties. Eighteenth-century men and women none the less had to go on playing their part in what was called the divine plan. The few clues we have suggest that Mozart lived in unshowy acceptance of that plan, and took part in the ritual and sacraments of his arm of the Christian church, anyhow at vital moments. He was so far committed to that arm as to write, from Paris in 1778, that he would take a post only in a Catholic country. Both he and Leopold mocked individual clergy, not to mention their ruling archbishop; their allegiance was to the faith and the church, whatever its officers.

To a young Catholic composer the church gave ready employment; to Mozart in Salzburg, writing for it was part of his duties. That meant writing some numbers, choral especially, in a 'learned' polyphonic style, though others might be in the 'galant' style used for all sorts of music, comic opera included.

The 'learned' style went back, through the recent Salzburg composer Johann Ernst Eberlin, to the Vienna-based J. J. Fux, author of a famous treatise – ultimately to the masters of the renaissance. Not that the young Mozart had much knowledge of renaissance music with its flowing polyphony; when, at nineteen, he sent a 'learned' motet of his to the scholar Padre Martini – the well-wisher who had helped him through the Philharmonic Academy's examination at Bologna – Martini sent back two-edged praise of this 'modern music'.

Mozart's encounter, after his move to Vienna, with the work of J. S. Bach and Handel has been made much of by some, played down by others. He was indeed much struck, adapted five Bach fugues for string quartet, reorchestrated *Messiah* to fit contemporary taste, and directed this and other Handel adaptations in Baron van Swieten's private concerts. Unsurprisingly, he now thought the Eberlin works he had studied as a boy 'far too trivial to deserve a place beside Handel and Bach'; for a time not only he but Constanze too revelled in fugues. Mozart was none the less schooled from childhood in the 'learned' style: counterpoint was all in the day's work.

In his early years the south German choral and orchestral mass flourished. It used not just winds and strings but, often, trumpets and drums – apt for 'making a joyful noise unto the Lord' rather than for introspection. South German churches of the mid eighteenth century used all the arts to revel in a piety of wonder and delight. Rococo virtuosity in their architecture and decoration still puts off the austere; others value them among of the jewels of Europe. The music that went on in them ran foul of the gothicising nineteenth century. It can still strike some people as too cheerful: faith ought not to have such a good time.

The boy Mozart had occasion to write a few such masses in Vienna and Salzburg, as well as shorter sacred pieces there and elsewhere; the best known is the brilliant motet 'Exsultate, jubilate' (K. 165), written in Milan in 1773 for a castrato to show off in church the powers of ornate singing he was already demonstrating in *Lucio Silla*. With Wolfgang's job at Salzburg in the next few years went more masses – at least until 1776. In that year he complained to Padre Martini that under the new archbishop a mass with all its sections fully orchestrated must not last more than three-quarters of an hour (some were shorter still; Colloredo also wanted audible words, unencumbered with musical display). Mozart clearly hankered after a post with greater opportunities, and hoped Martini would put one in his way. Yet the short Salzburg masses reached more people than any of his other compositions: many churches within a hundred miles or so copied and performed them. They were his nearest approach to popular music.

What Mozart was driving at in these works we can best see from the 'Coronation' Mass in C (K. 317) and the Solemn Vespers 'de Confessore' (K. 339), each written for Salzburg in his last years there, 1779 and 1780. 'Driving' is the word for the short mass, majestic headlong power its characteristic. The Credo keeps up the momentum even when it slows down for a moment of gravitas at the Incarnation, of sorrow at the Crucifixion. So does the traditionally mild Benedictus. Only the Agnus Dei, a gracious, wide-ranging solo, makes a pause in a resounding sonority often filled out with horns, trumpets, trombones, and drums. No wonder the mass was later played at a coronation, and misnamed after it.

In the vespers the contrapuntal passages for chorus and orchestra may be on the solemn, even (in the showily contrapuntal 'Laudate pueri') on the sombre side of grand; the effect, all the same, is not of depth but of gladness. The work opens in brilliance and finishes in splendour; before the 'Magnificat' that closes it the 'Laudate dominum' unfolds a seamless, gentle melody for soprano, consolatory without being mystical.

In late Salzburg works like these, Mozart – so Alfred Einstein thought – deliberately irked his employer by here and there going against orders and indulging in 'stormy solemnity': he had to utter something the archbishop's rational liturgy could not contain. That may tell us why, in Munich at the time of *Idomeneo* in 1781, he wished to perform one of his sacred works: the Elector Karl Theodor, who for the past three years had denied him a job, might yield to the power of mass and opera combined. If, as seems likely, the Kyrie in D minor was written with this in mind, it shows that here as in *Idomeneo* Mozart worked spiritually at full throttle: scored for utmost splendour, its plea for mercy is stern, dark, yet open to the transcendent. Einstein thought the mastery of structure and of detailed writing 'enough to make one fall on one's knees'. Musicologists no longer fall on their knees, and neither (if he was the person addressed) did the Elector.

Vienna, where Mozart lived from 1781, held out still fewer openings for church music. Joseph II's policy, very like Colloredo's, had cut down services and the use of instruments, besides doing away with one monastic church after another; it would later take a stand against choral singing. Neither Mozart nor Haydn was to write any sacred music for the Austrian lands until after Joseph's death in 1790. Oddly, there remained Salzburg – a Benedictine church there, outside the archbishop's control. On 26 October 1783, during Wolfgang's one trip home, he and Constanze performed the Mass in C minor. For reasons still obscure, it was unfinished; he was never to complete it.

'I made the promise in my heart of hearts' – Wolfgang had written to his father on 4 January – to celebrate his and his wife's visit with a mass; at that time he had written 'half' of it. The mass was to give thanks for Constanze's having come safely through her pregnancy (or through an earlier illness) – essentially for their being together, a condition imaged by her performing one of the two soprano solo parts while he either played the organ or led from the violin. The dimensions and temper of the work suggest an aim more far-reaching. If Mozart had completed it on the scale of the parts he did write, it would have been as long as the Mass in B minor in which J. S. Bach had summed up a lifetime's devotional music-making. Like that work, though in other terms, it was heaven-scaling.

Mozart completed the Kyrie and Gloria, the first part of the Credo, enough of the Sanctus for it to be reconstructed, and the Benedictus; he never wrote the latter part of the Credo or the Agnus Dei. Just what was performed at Salzburg we do not know. The Kyrie and Gloria Mozart later (1785) adapted into an oratorio for Vienna on the theme of David's repentance. Presumably he saw no chance of ever having the mass sung there; that would tell us why he did not bother to complete it, though not why he left it incomplete in the first place. There may have been local circumstances we do not know about.

Even in its truncated form the mass tells us more about its composer's relation to God than do his earlier letters. That relation is not quite straightforward.

For Bach the individual – composer or hearer – lived without question as part of a spiritual world beyond time; experience of God was at once collective and personal, and music was to deepen it. In his mass Mozart shapes a grand framework within which the voices take now one view, now another of the tremendous events they sing. At the 'Qui tollis' for double chorus, with its relentless chromatic lunges, the freight of the world's evil bears down on us; Christ – the words say – lifts it, but according to the music it has not yet happened. When the words announce peace on earth to men of goodwill and, later, bless him who comes in the name of the Lord, an uneasy, almost questioning note slips in. Yet the Kyrie, alternately stern and elegiac, launches the mass on a note of certainty; the mighty homophonic shout 'Jesus Christ', leading to the athletic fugue on 'with the holy spirit', confirms it; the early part of the Credo, in the spirit of the 'Coronation' Mass, drives its tough ostinato along without bothering to imitate the descent from heaven it confidently asserts.

The solo voice utters, at 'Christe eleison' and in two arias; we do not know which of them Constanze sang. From the 'Laudamus te', a coloratura aria of Italian type, we gather that abstract beauty is, for God, praise enough. The more elaborate 'Et incarnatus est', a concerto for voice, flute, oboe, and bassoon to be sung at that point in the Credo, used to be thought of as operatic by those who disliked its kinship with the windblown angels in the South German churches of its day, innocent in painted stucco and gilt. It brings the good news in the most caressing manner imaginable, to now lilting, now leaping melodies berthed on the tenderest of accompaniments, and soothes on through unresolved repetitions ('-tu-us est') as though too enchanted to let go. Mozart left it in draft, complete but for the string parts. Incarnation is a mystery, as much in any new-born child as in the son of God: if Constanze sang this, she sang it two months after her and Wolfgang's firstborn had died.

We would be rash to draw conclusions from an unfinished work. As it stands, the mass bursts the banks of late eighteenth-century convention; it deploys a rousing variety and grandeur; praise for a

14 Ignaz Günther, 'The Annunciation'. This painted wood sculpture of 1764 was
the last word in a South German tradition of religious art that combined
utmost refinement and grace with real feeling, a combination found in the 'Et
Incarnatus' from Mozart's mightiest religious work, the Mass in C Minor.

transcendent God reaches high, yet some unevenness of tone hints that the composer was not altogether at ease with his task. At a conscious level, Mozart perhaps intended nothing so much as an outlet for powers Vienna would not let him use.

Just over a year after the performance of the Mass in C minor, on 14 December 1784, Mozart became an apprentice member of one of the eight Vienna Masonic lodges, named 'Beneficence'. Within three and a half weeks he was admitted as a journeyman to the second of the (then) three degrees of the Masonic 'craft', in a ceremony at the related, more important 'True Concord' lodge, and he ended as a master, perhaps within a further week. He was to be a Mason for the rest of his life – after Joseph II's reorganisation of the lodges, as a member of the 'New Crowned Hope'. Did Freemasonry give him a new spiritual understanding such as to weaken his Christian belief? Did it lead him to question further the existing order of church and state?

Freemasonry in the late eighteenth century was in the first place a sociable movement, a loose chain of clubs where men could meet on an equal footing even though some were nobles and others minor gentry, merchants, officials, or professionals. The 'inquisitive women' named in the title of Goldoni's comedy of 1753 longed to know what their men were up to at their secret club; after many extravagant guesses, they crept in to find the men busy with a slap-up dinner. The clubbiness of Freemasonry was important: it signalled that men were no longer content to mix chiefly with their own class. They might still have to do so on public occasions, but here they could relax.

According to the statutes of every lodge they were not to discuss politics or religion. The lodges did, however, carry on a ritual of their own in a language of symbolic words, images, and gestures, a serious matter in continental countries where both church and state claimed exclusive power.

In their known statements, for example in the words of the songs Mozart was to compose, Masons gave voice to benevolence towards

fellow-men and a generalised praise of God, seen as the 'great archi-
tect' or 'soul' of the universe; they spoke of the need to uphold virtue,
loyalty, brotherhood, and charity and follow the 'light of truth'. Much
of this was the common coin of 'enlightened' thought.

The late eighteenth century, however, was also a time when more
esoteric ideas were about, of philosophical or semi-religious cast – in
part a coming into view of once obscure lines of thought, in part a sign
that Christian orthodoxy was beginning to lose hold. Alchemy – the
centuries-old endeavour to arrive at treasure more inward than
material gold – was not spent. Ancient 'mysteries', those of the
Egyptians in particular, interested some. Notions of universal happiness, to be attained by the use of reason and a more equal sharing out
of wealth, informed a Bavarian secret society called the Illuminati.
Some Freemasons held these ideas, and the Illuminati, anticipating
later groups, wished to promote theirs by infiltrating the lodges.

Did Mozart share in the esoteric interests of some Masons? The
chief evidence is a set of 'Zoroastrian riddles' he devised and handed
out at a carnival masquerade in 1786; he later sent them to his father.
Both riddles and eastern cults such as Zoroastrianism were fashionable, but Mozart's set is not so much arcane as bawdy; thus 'One can
possess me without seeing me' means 'horns'. The riddles confirm
Mozart's delight in both obscene jokes and the play of language.
Whether they can bear the weight of psychoanalytical interpretation
placed on them by Maynard Solomon is an open question; what is certain is that they do not show Mozart delving into the occult.

Can we then say that Mozart shared the radical views of some
Masons? Since the Illuminati in particular can be seen as forerunners
of communism, some writers have looked for evidence that Mozart
was involved with them or, more generally, held radical ideas and welcomed revolution when it broke out in the Low Countries and France.
There is, however, no direct evidence. The indirect evidence is weak. It
depends on association: some Vienna Freemasons are thought to
have been influenced by the Illuminati; Mozart was a member of the
same lodge. This is wishful thinking rather than proof.

Mozart, we have seen, felt keenly the absurdity of privilege; he knew his talents had earned him a high place, and resented great people's being able to deny it him. It is not surprising that he should have welcomed membership of a club where he could talk as an equal with some of the greatest nobles in the land. He used Masonic signs in correspondence with fellow members, and composed music for performance in the lodges, most of it in two bursts, one soon after his admission, the other just before his death – the period when he also wrote The Magic Flute, a work that embodies masonic ideas and some Masonic ritual devices. Freemasonry apart, he admired Britain (where he had lived aged seven to nine) as the home of liberty – another commonplace among the 'enlightened', though questioned by advanced republicans and democrats. That is all we know. Assertions that he was a committed radical are speculative.

Those who make such assertions read back into the 1780s the part Masonry came to play on the continent after the French Revolution. Alarmed governments suppressed it (in Vienna, four years after Mozart's death); Freemasons, when they reappeared in the nineteenth century, by and large identified themselves with anticlerical liberalism, some with republicanism and democracy.

In the 1780s, however, many high government officials and leading clergy were members of the Vienna lodges: 'it was clearly possible', the historian Derek Beales has written, 'to be both a Mason and a pillar of the Catholic Establishment'. Among other members were Mozart's noble patrons Count Thun and Count Esterhazy, his publishers Artaria and Torricella, his printer-landlord J. T. von Trattner, his favourite tenor Adamberger, Leopold Mozart (admitted during his 1785 visit), Haydn (who did not bother to attend), bankers, officers, doctors, merchants, an actor, a bookseller, an apothecary – a virtual cross-section of the upper and middle classes. Attempts to identify them with the programme of the Illuminati are hazardous; so far as they were politically inclined they supported Joseph II's reform of the church. Early in 1785 Joseph rewarded the effective leader of the movement in Vienna, the mineralogist Ignaz

15 Initiation of an apprentice at a Vienna Masonic Lodge: anonymous oil painting

von Born, for his discovery of a process that increased miners' safety.
Mozart helped one of the lodges to celebrate by writing a cantata,
'The Masons' Joy'.

Nor did Joseph the Wise (as the words of the cantata termed him)
unambiguously round on the Masons when, in December of that year,
he cut down the number of lodges and had their members officially
listed. In a country where little was meant to happen without the government's knowing about it, regulation was a kind of recognition.
The Masons may have been shaken – some of the more esoterically
minded dropped out, as Joseph had intended – but most carried on.
The emperor, they could reassure themselves, was of their frame of
mind: ten years earlier he had thrown open his private suburban park
and inscribed on the gateway 'Pleasure ground dedicated to the
People, by one who esteems them'; he still dressed and behaved with
the greatest simplicity and went on imposing church and educational
reform. Even when the Netherlands revolution brought new strain,
Joseph would have nothing to do with a proposal to infiltrate an

alleged Masonic revolutionary conspiracy. This was in late 1787, the very time when he bestowed a sinecure on the Freemason Mozart.

If we interrogate the music Mozart wrote for his brothers in the lodges, we get a disconcerting reply. As the Marxist scholar Georg Knepler – keen to bring out Mozart's radical sympathies – has honestly acknowledged, these compositions, 'all but one, never rise above a middling artistic level'; some are 'banal'. 'Four-square' and 'routine' also fit these songs, duos, and cantatas; some of the choruses (male only, of course) evoke a German glee club. Knepler's explanation – these works were written for people who had little or no musical grounding or sensibility – does not fit what we know of some lodge brothers; 'The Masons' Joy' was written for the admired professional Adamberger. Mozart used customary Masonic devices – thirds, threefold structures, slurred notes, 'knocking at the door' rhythms, the key of E♭ – but seems not to have put his heart into the job.

Knepler's one exception, the *Masonic Funeral Music* (K. 477), was written in 1785 for meetings to commemorate two aristocratic lodge brothers, one a ruling prince, the other a high official; neither death can have touched Mozart personally. Its texture is heavy with deep wind instruments – bassoon, basset horn, horn (to which Mozart later added a contrabassoon) as well as oboe, clarinet, and strings. It works a sonority more than literally profound, a colour at once dark and glowing. Framed by a C minor slow march, a middle panel of chorale variations in E♭ lifts a voice plangent yet serene. A hint of Christian supplication – a fragment of chant traditionally used in the Miserere of the Requiem mass – runs athwart the Masonic symbols and the Masonic equanimity. The whole thing takes just over four minutes; the end resolves from gloom into a C major chord; the indigo vault bleaches into open sky. This extraordinary work holds in balance sorrow and peace; men's souls can face death because they hold to a ruling power not themselves, but in that power dwells no transcendence, no personality; Christ's face is nowhere.

Writing for instruments rather than for earnest Masonic voices may have set free Mozart's creative powers: the *Funeral Music* looks forward to some of the works of his last phase. In the years 1784–88 we can glimpse his experience of the spirit mostly in his secular works.

Some have found it in tormented minor-key works like the piano concerto in D minor (K. 466), first performed in February 1785. To do so is tempting but probably fallacious – the outcome of listening across the roar of the self-dramatising nineteenth century. Mozart could be poignant in major-key works. He could also create such a masterpiece as the piano concerto in C minor (K. 491, finished in March 1786), which keeps up the tension more thoroughgoingly than does the D minor concerto and works its ideas more fully and explicitly; yet its total gesture is of a heroism that seeks no monument. Mozart, in any case, tended to pair a stressful work with another more relaxed or affirmative – the D minor concerto with that in C (K. 467), the string quintets in C and in G minor (K. 515–16), the two last symphonies in G minor and in C (K. 550–1) – just as, in the operas of 1786–87, *The Marriage of Figaro* and *Don Giovanni*, an opening on a possible heaven or hell will yield to the concerns, laughable, erotic, or crass, of everyday humanity.

The works of these years do speak in Mozart's personal voice. We do well to listen for it in the single work, yet also for the balance he achieved, much of the time, either within a single work or within a pair or series. If a mood, a gesture is unquestionable we should heed it, with reservations: Mozart meant it, but he meant a great deal else besides.

His outward personal life affords few clues. People close to him died, but the deaths of his and Constanze's children – three of them from 1786 to 1789 – left no record of the parents' feelings. Leopold Mozart's death in 1787, we have seen, led Wolfgang into borrowed 'philosophical' acceptance. He and his father had grown apart, perhaps more than adult sons and their parents generally did, though they still wrote and exchanged news; two years had gone by since Leopold had visited him and Constanze, it seems without incident, and had gathered from Haydn proof of his son's genius. Now Leopold was dying, that son, however 'emancipated', was bound to be shaken.

Did he express himself more individually in music than in his letter on death? We do not know. A possible memorial, Alan Tyson has suggested, is the well-known serenade for strings (really a brief chamber suite) *Eine kleine Nachtmusik* (K. 525), written a couple of months after Leopold's death – the quintessence, a trifle ghostly, of the divertimenti Mozart had composed in his father's shadow at Salzburg. If Tyson is right in his shrewd guess, Wolfgang absorbed the death into music whose self-contained beauty fends off interpretation.

One might suppose that a tumult of feeling about Leopold's mortal illness accounted for the string quintet in G minor (K. 516), one of Wolfgang's greatest and most tragic works: he entered it in his register on 16 May 1787, twelve days before his father's death. Dates, in fact, all but rule out a connection.[1] At most, knowledge of what was about to happen may have shaped the end of the quintet. That, if true, would show a great deal about where Mozart's spirit was tending.

The G minor stands paired with the C major quintet (K. 515), written at the same time. Mozart, it appears, planned a set which he would offer to amateur subscribers, but when, a year later, he advertised these two, bulked out with a transcription (K. 406) of the C minor wind serenade (K. 388), the scheme failed; he eventually sold them to a publisher.

Both quintets are built on a large scale. Charles Rosen, in his penetrating study, writes of the C major: 'Mozart discovers the secret of Beethoven's dimensions.' He does it by a use of motivic fragments held within tonal solidity, achieved by staying in the tonic far longer than usual; this creates tension 'while remaining at the extreme point of resolution'. The opening Allegro thus combines 'breadth and majesty' with 'lyric intensity'. This Allegro makes a complex argument at once grand and exhilarating. The Andante's dialogue of violin and viola, now yearning, now suave, shows tenderness may be a spacious emotion. The Minuet keeps close to it in mood until the trio brings in a sliding, lilting tune that might be an ironic device of Mahler's (his, though, would go on four times as long; here it is a passing joke). Abounding melodic ideas in the finale – friendly, vigorous, gracious – take us through one transforming adventure after another. Life rewards exploration; the Lord (if we admit the words Haydn was to set in *The Creation*) is 'great in his might'.

The G minor works the same means of tonal solidity in a wholly contrasting mood. The opening, disturbed over a quaver pulse, is (Rosen again) of 'a chromatic bitterness and insistence that can still shock by the naked force of its anguish'. The Minuet keeps up the tension, with, in the opening bars, a grinding contrast twice leading to a *forte* chord like a repeated pang and, in the trio, only a fleeting glimpse of sky. From the very start of the Adagio ma non troppo, fragmented motives stammer, mope in isolation; the rhythmic pulse alters, never settling for long; song-like melodies appear, but they dwell morbidly on suffering, or suggest tears, or, at most, acceptance of fate; a high one offers consolation so thin as to be none at all; the last phrase, in a quiet upward leap, seems to say 'finish'.

Worse is to come. The Adagio introduction to the finale, according to Rosen,

> even surpasses the other movements in its open use of direct
> expressive symbolism: the sobbing rhythm of the inner strings, the
> sighing appoggiaturas, the harsh expressive dissonances, the aria at
> once sustained without end and continuously broken, the parlando
> insistence on one note, the unceasing chromatic movement.
> Nothing closer to ultimate despair has ever been imagined . . .

Some have invoked Gethsemane: the agony in the garden. There, Christ at length said: 'Not as I will, but as thou wilt.' Mozart stops, then picks up again with an Allegro in G major and in rondo form.

Opinions differ on what this says and how it should be played. Cheered or disconsolate? Bright or subdued? What is certain is that the agony is over. God's will is reasonable, after all. The instruments talk on in lines now simple, now contrapuntal, but the pulse is steady, the recurrent theme almost jaunty. We can understand this in various ways. It disappoints some: not enough, surely, to purge all that suffering? Or we may say: the classical spirit in the arts demands formal resolution, and this resolves what went before. Or, finally, we may hear in the quintet as a whole what the apparition in *Little Gidding* told T. S. Eliot about remorse:

> From wrong to wrong the exasperated spirit
> Proceeds, unless restored by that refining fire
> Where you must move in measure, like a dancer.

The final Allegro does 'move in measure', with the disciplined cheer of purgatory. There is an everlasting No, but also, if we listen, an everlasting Yes. Perhaps, for reasons hidden from us, Mozart in this work overbalanced towards the No; but he heard the Yes, and moved with it.

The Yes speaks even in the work often said to show tension unresolved, the G minor symphony (K. 550). It was one of three he wrote in the summer of 1788, falling between the E♭ (K. 549) and the C major or 'Jupiter' (K. 551). All soon became famous, but in 1788 Mozart no doubt intended them as something he could make money with now that the Vienna audience – perhaps he too – had had enough of piano concertos; there is evidence that he had concerts lined up. At all events he did not write his greatest symphonies in a void; nor could he have known that they were to be his last. Nor, finally, do the symphonies as a group show the financial strain Mozart was under: with the outbreak of the Turkish war in February the bad times had started, and by June or July so had the series of begging letters to his friend Michael Puchberg.

What the three symphonies did show – with their fellow the 'Prague' symphony in D (K. 504), performed in late 1786 – was a new departure in the genre. The old symphony as overture or entertainment was no more. In these four, and in the symphonies Haydn was to write for London in the 1790s, music aimed at a discourse, perhaps of profound import, at all events fully thought out and worked out; to hear it properly you had to listen with care.

Since Mozart wrote it, people have heard the G minor symphony in widely varying ways. To contemporaries, the adventurous key changes in the outer movements must have sounded extreme, yet a couple of Romantic generations later Schumann heard only 'Grecian lightness and grace'. Modern critics tend to speak of 'inexorableness', 'neuroticism', 'passion, violence, and grief'. The final bar, still in the minor – an obstinacy unusual at the time – drives in a last nail.

Or does it? The work can sound not so much inexorable as keenly ambiguous. It too hears both the No and the Yes – in the universe, and in that other universe, the self; Mozart's experience of earth, heaven, and hell shows in the structure both of the symphony as a whole and of individual movements.

This is not to deny – though the odd conductor tries to – the merciless drive from the start of the opening Molto allegro, with its anapaestic rhythm prompted by an offbeat whisper in the strings. This temper, weirdly implacable, rules the first movement, the fierce main sections of the Minuet, and the Allegro assai finale. In its menace there is order of the highest kind, the more fearful because the symphony does without the intimidatory aid of trumpets and drums; the mutations we undergo in the development section of the first movement form an organised tempest. The structure of the last movement is so decisively regular as to attain formal resolution; its placing of 'the square upon the oblong' fulfils the classical task of rounding off (and therefore denying the ego the unbounded self-expression it craves) without conceding anything to heart's ease. Only the E♭ major Andante and the Trio envision a world where order is beauty, calm, and delight.

Yet the contrast is stronger within the two outer movements than between them and the Andante and Trio. These gentler sections concern themselves with an order human beings might imagine, even attain, on earth. In the recapitulation of the Andante Mozart runs the consolatory falling phrase with its demi-semiquaver train above another, song-like melody; two human ways of loving go on together, with no need to overcome or merge. At the end of the movement a single chord with appoggiatura speaks a clear-eyed farewell.

In the outer movements, though, the uncanny enters with second subjects whose ethereal or mysterious character is flicked in by limpid woodwind textures. Counterpoint too eavesdrops: at times in the first movement a bass line muses, arcane, while the implacable discourse goes on overhead. Fierce outcries in that same movement give way to a benison dropping down, this time from heaven; or outcry and blessing go on at once. Just before the end the blessing recurs, offers a glimpse of salvation; a like chance hovers just before the symphony ends.

A few years after Mozart had completed the G minor symphony, a more radical artist, stirred by the great events in France, wrote *The Marriage of Heaven and Hell*. William Blake there abolished the boundary dividing soul and body, will and morality, men and women and God: 'All deities reside in the human breast'; and that breast holds the infinite if only we would see it, and its energy 'is Eternal Delight' if only we would unshackle it. Here at its purest was the Romantic vision of the human mind as the sole universe, imaging, shaping, determining the outer world. In Blake it could make for piercing sweetness and depth of understanding. In some later human beings it could breed monsters, as the mind fed on itself without care for any reality beyond itself, natural or supernatural. It is a vision we have cause at once to prize and to distrust.

Mozart moves towards the Romantic vision as he lets the iridescent, at times appalling emotions of his life and ours move in and out of his finest work; but he remains conscious of an Other, holds himself ultimately ready to 'move in measure, like a dancer' and shape his creation not by his own will alone. The G minor symphony, high point of a line running through his work, holds in a perfect frame anxiety that is visited by knowledge of blessedness, yet remains anxiety still. It is once again modern, and shows why Mozart is our contemporary.

6 The last phase

Two things happened early in 1788 that were to give Mozart a hard time; neither was of his making. War broke out with Turkey, and the emperor for the first time, allowed opera in Lent.

Writers on Mozart have stressed the ill effects of the war: it went badly at first, brought the usual plagues of vast expenditure and inflation – compounded by bad harvests – sent the emperor and some of the aristocracy off to the front while other noble families retrenched, and, after a burst of patriotism, settled on Vienna an atmosphere of alternate hysteria and gloom. Mozart joined in the patriotic send-off – he wrote music for two war songs and named two dances after successful actions – but his audience was in part dispersed.

The other change has had less notice. Joseph II had begun to open up the old theatre calendar, long punctuated by closures during religious holidays and fasts; it happened all over Europe as part of the secularising of daily life, but he pioneered it, and now, as a final measure, he opened up Lent throughout the Austrian lands. Opera was the genre the audience cared about most. While it was shut down in Lent other forms of music-making flourished – oratorio, but also public and private concerts such as Mozart had given; in the good years 1782–86 Lent was his busiest time, with removal men continually lugging his piano in and out of the flat. Now concerts dwindled – on top of what seems to have been a falling off in his own appeal.

Opera too, though allowed a longer season, fell victim to wartime cuts in expenditure. The German opera closed (after the 'national' experiment at the Burgtheater it had been hived off to another theatre) and Joseph nearly closed the Italian opera as well; his second thoughts were to make possible *Così fan tutte*.

That, however, did not happen until the winter of 1789–90. Two and a half years earlier Mozart was already in difficulties – and they got worse. By his own account he was in deep trouble all the way from June 1788 to June 1791. In the last few months of his life things got better: the war was ending, fashion began to change, he wrote two operas. Yet he died still owing money.

About all this we are ill informed. The years 1789–90 are among the worst documented of Mozart's life. For knowledge of his debts we have to rely chiefly on his begging letters to the merchant Michael Puchberg, his friend, brother Mason, and creditor. Not all the letters may have survived; other creditors have left little or no trace. We have indications, but no full account. At least once Mozart resorted to a pawnbroker – and then asked Puchberg for a loan on the security of the tickets; another time he threatened to go to what would now be called loan sharks.

The first sign of trouble was Wolfgang's and Constanze's move in April 1787 from their grand flat to a cheap lodging in the suburb of Landstrasse. They moved back to the inner city in December, probably encouraged by Wolfgang's appointment early that month as 'chamber musician' to the emperor, at 800 florins a year. By June 1788, however, they still owed some of their Landstrasse rent and the owner was being 'importunate'; they had to move to yet another suburb. To Puchberg (who bailed him out) Wolfgang made out that the new rooms were not only cheaper but, in the warm months, '*more pleasant, as I have a garden too*'.

Soon after the original April 1787 move Leopold Mozart had died. Two months later Wolfgang settled with his brother-in-law, Nannerl's husband, for 1,000 florins as his share of the estate; he insisted that they should be Vienna florins, worth about 1,200

16 Mozart, Leipzig, 1789: silverpoint by Doris Stock. This miniature portrait is one of the few to suggest both a good likeness and an insight into character.

Salzburg florins. According to the biographer Maynard Solomon, he was almost certainly cheated out of an amount several times as large, which went to Nannerl, probably both before and after Leopold's death.

To reach this conclusion Solomon assumes first that Leopold made a notable profit on the family's tours in 1762–73, and secondly that he hung on to it. Neither is obvious. Most of the earnings may have gone on expenses. Some well-known musicians in the eighteenth and early nineteenth centuries made a lot of money and then lost it – not always through gambling or improvidence: before the coming of a regular stock exchange, investments, even in state securities, easily went wrong (not that they are foolproof today). We should also have to assume that Wolfgang's father lied to him in 1778 when he wrote that he was having to go into debt and give lessons to support the tour to Paris. That seems unlikely: in a town like Salzburg, Wolfgang would have found out on his return; the very pedantry that made Leopold a heavy father goes ill with lying.

We have no means of knowing whether the division of the estate was fair, and no grounds for supposing it was not, at least in rough terms. (Mozart used his and Nannerl's old friend Franz d'Yppold as his representative – something of a guarantee – but, in his urgent need for a lump sum, may have taken less than he could have got by waiting for the assets to be fully realised.)

Mozart's troubles were real. What is hard to gauge is how far he was mired in debt, whether the debt got steadily worse or fluctuated, and how it touched his inmost feelings.

'Good God! I am coming to you not with thanks but with fresh entreaties! Instead of paying my debts I am asking for more money!' So he wrote to Puchberg on 14 July 1789, apparently a year after his last request (but there may be letters missing in between). He had been ill, hence unable to work; Constanze was ill; he had advertised an offer to hold subscription concerts in his rooms, but in a fortnight had collected only one name, Baron van Swieten's. All the same, he had prospects: he was writing six string quartets for the King of Prussia, and six easy piano sonatas for the king's daughter. He therefore pleaded with his brother Mason to save him for ruin. 'Oh God!' he added in a postscript, 'I can hardly bring myself to despatch this letter! – and yet I must! . . . For God's sake only forgive me, only forgive me! – and – Adieu!'

More begging letters went to Puchberg – three days later, in December, on 20 January 1790, 20 February, March–April (three letters), May (two letters), June, and August, then again in June 1791. At times Mozart asked for a large sum that would free him from anxiety and let him get on with his work – up to 2,000 florins, to be gradually repaid with interest. In August 1790, however, 'the smallest sum would be very welcome just now'; Puchberg sent him ten florins. He had earlier sent amounts ranging from twenty-five to 300 florins; by and large he met specific requests at once, but he never provided the large sum that was meant to give his friend a breathing-space.

What are we to make of this? Puchberg's response suggests that he wished to help in emergencies. Whether he charged interest and at what rate we do not know, but in this relationship at least he was not a usurer; Mozart made him a present of a trio, perhaps the magnificent, deeply serious Divertimento in E♭ (K. 563). For all that, Puchberg had no intention of providing a capital sum – perhaps because he knew his man and thought it would run through his fingers. (If Mozart was a gambler Puchberg's behaviour would be readily explained.)

Mozart used emotive language: 'I have been living in such misery', 'rescue me just this time from my horrible situation', 'tears [of gratitude] prevent me from completing the picture!' Did it fully engage him? The biographer Wolfgang Hildesheimer thought not: Mozart, in his view, could beg and yet remain detached; his real commitment was to music. This may be shrewder than some of Hildesheimer's other guesses. Mozart could adapt himself to his correspondent. He could be ardent for German national opera when writing to a German nationalist, and at other times prefer Italian opera: ingratiation – a social instinct – running to temporary enthusiasm, rather than lying. There is also some doubt whether the Prussian royal family had commissioned him to write the pieces he held out as future security. He completed (and sold for publication) only three of the six quartets and one of the six sonatas. All the same, even if he piled it on somewhat in his begging letters, they cannot have been pleasant for a man to write who so valued his own 'honour'.

Besides Puchberg, Mozart drew on at least three major creditors, the merchant Heinrich Lackenbacher, the publisher Franz Anton

Hoffmeister, and the aristocrat Prince Karl Lichnowsky. Dealings with the first two are unclear. From Lackenbacher he borrowed, according to a promissory note bearing a conventional date (1 October 1790, when he was not in Vienna), 1,000 florins for two years at 5 per cent a year. From Hoffmeister he may have got security for this loan, or a separate loan designed to pay off Lackenbacher (or another creditor who was owed 1,000 florins) and leave something over; either way he was to pay Hoffmeister in new music, so, as he wrote airily to Constanze, 'I need never repay the sum . . . everything will be quite in order.'[1] Lichnowsky (later Beethoven's patron) got a court order a month before Mozart's death to have a 1,435-florin debt repaid, if need be out of Mozart's salary, but did not enforce it. The origin of the debt is unknown; it may have arisen when the two men went together to Berlin in 1789.

We know of a few minor creditors, such as a haberdasher, and, probably, at least one undocumented major creditor who was still lending money in July 1791. Mozart was indeed in trouble. Yet he was not without resource.

Even in Vienna – the only place, he told Puchberg, where 'fate is so much against me' – he appears to have given one more clutch of subscription concerts in 1788. Even in the bad year 1789 he continued to arrange Handel works for Baron van Swieten; late that year he was commissioned to write *Così fan tutte*, and wrote the lovely, melancholy clarinet quintet (K. 581) for his friend Anton Stadler to perform. He sold various pieces to copyists and publishers, mostly dances and songs or arias, but also the string quintets for which he had been unable to find subscribers.

In the still more dreadful year 1790 he was 'obliged', he told Puchberg, to 'give away . . . for a mere song' the so-called Prussian string quartets (K. 575, 589–90) – most likely to a copyist; they were engraved and published eighteen months later, no doubt for a suitable fee. He still arranged Handel works for van Swieten. By May he had two pupils and was willing to take on six more – a desperate measure, for he had earlier complained that pupils used up time and energy. He agreed to write pieces for a mechanical organ with 'high-pitched' and 'childish' pipes, commemorating a hero of the war.

About the first, the Adagio and Allegro in F minor (K. 594), he told Constanze that he was doing it 'to slip a few ducats into the hand of my dear little wife': 'as it is a kind of composition which I detest, I have unfortunately not been able to finish it. I compose a bit of it every day – but I break off now and then, as I get bored . . . But I still hope that I shall force myself gradually to finish it.' He did; in fact he wrote two more pieces for the same instrument, one of them (the fantasy in F minor, K. 608) a masterful polyphonic display. The jobbing composer in Mozart had not given up.

All along he had a sheet-anchor – the salary Joseph II had granted him. It was kept on after Joseph's death in February 1790; Mozart hoped for a time that the new emperor, Joseph's brother Leopold II, might take him on as first or, more likely, deputy court composer, but nothing came of it: Leopold – who as grand duke of Tuscany had heard the boy Wolfgang – was even more wedded than his brother to the reigning Italian style. Mozart may not even have got round to petitioning for a job.

There remained the chance of a foreign tour. Mozart had thought of going to England in 1787 with the returning prima donna of the *Figaro* company, Nancy Storace, her brother the composer Stephen Storace, the tenor Michael Kelly, and his own composition student Thomas Attwood, all of them friends; he had got as far as asking his father to take charge of his and Constanze's two children (Karl Thomas and another who shortly died aged one month).

Leopold Mozart declined; the parents, he commented sarcastically to Nannerl, 'could go off and travel – they might even die – or remain in England – and I should have to run off after them with the children'. This was unfeeling but, as usual, shrewd. It was one thing for Leopold to bring up Nannerl's child, as he was doing – not an outlandish arrangement at the time – with the mother living in the next town, another to take on children whose parents would be a thousand miles away, exposed to the usual eighteenth-century hazards of illness and the uncertainties of a musical career. Leopold also advised Wolfgang, rightly, that England was expensive and summer was no time to get there; in any case Stephen Storace would surely write the opera for the next London season (he did).

Why did Mozart not go to England on his own, or imitate Leopold and take his children with him? The distance and the risk were, at that time, great; he may have known that his organising capacity did not match his father's. Late in 1790 the manager of the Italian opera in London, Robert Bray O'Reilly, offered him £300 to spend six months there, write two operas, and be free to give concerts; nothing came of it – just as well, for O'Reilly was a catspaw for unscrupulous owners who burnt down the opera house.

A little later still, in December, the impresario who took Haydn off to London on his first triumphant journey perhaps invited Mozart as well. (Haydn later thought he remembered Mozart saying with tears in his eyes that they would probably never meet again; this may be true, but when a genius dies young such recollections easily spring up.) Mozart liked now and then to speak and write a few words of English; he liked to meet English people, one of whom, a music publisher's employee, remembered him 'rather melancholy until he spoke, when his expression became animated and amused and his eyes . . . full of kind concern in our doings . . .' Mozart in England at the height of his powers is an intriguing might-have-been.

Instead he undertook two journeys, one between 8 April and 4 June 1789 to Prague, Dresden, Leipzig, Potsdam, and Berlin, most of the time in the company of Prince Lichnowsky, the other between 23 September and about 10 November 1790 to Frankfurt for the coronation of Leopold II as emperor, then to Mainz, Mannheim, and Munich; this time he travelled in his own carriage with his brother-in-law the violinist Franz Hofer and a servant.

Both journeys cost money: keeping up with a nobleman must have been expensive; using a carriage of his own, while a convenience, was a stiff investment. Mozart clearly proposed to lay out money so as to make a great deal more. Yet, as on the 1777–79 tour to Paris, he reported home that he had made scarcely any.

The goal of the 1789 trip was the court of the Prussian king, Frederick the Great's successor Frederick William II, like him an amateur musician; he played the cello, and the first of the 'Prussian' quartets was meant for him. Mozart went first to the court at Potsdam, then back to Leipzig, where he had already stopped on the way – and happily improvised on Bach's organ in St Thomas's; on his second Leipzig visit he gave a concert, performing two piano concertos, the Fantasy in C minor, and, probably, two of the last four symphonies. He then went back north to Berlin.

We do not know what happened at Potsdam, because the letters Mozart told Constanze he had written from there are missing; we do know that on arrival he was seen not by the king but by his director of chamber music. Frederick the Great, forty-two years earlier, had said 'Gentlemen, old Bach is here' and had received the composer there and then; the evidence, however, is too fragmentary to prove that Mozart was snubbed. At some stage Mozart collected a sum equivalent to 700 florins; Frederick William's reported statement, after Mozart's death, that he had offered him a post is almost certainly untrue. From Berlin Mozart wrote that the queen wanted to hear him play – 'but I shan't make much money'; he ruled out a public concert there on the grounds that it would pay badly and the king did not wish him to give one, perhaps a way of saying that his whole reception was a comedown.

The Leipzig concert too had been 'a failure, as I always said it would be'. There is some – weak – corroboration from the author Friedrich Rochlitz, who was present; it is weak because Rochlitz fabricated stories about Mozart and was keen to show him as a misunderstood genius. Mozart, it seems, did best where he had fewest hopes – in Prague and Dresden on his way north. In Prague the impresario who had put on *Don Giovanni*, Domenico Guardasoni, offered him a contract for another opera (nothing came of it directly, because the troupe left for Warsaw). In Dresden Mozart caught up with his old friend the singer Josepha Duschek, gave a concert there with her and other musicians, performed a piano concerto for the Elector of Saxony – the 'Coronation' concerto in D (K. 537), designed to be brilliantly accessible – played at the Russian Minister's, and held an organ- and piano-playing competition with 'a pupil of a pupil of Bach's'. In both cities he was made much of, but earned, by his own account, no more than 'a handsome snuffbox'.

Much about the 1789 tour is unexplained. The lost letters (one of Constanze's and perhaps as many as four of Wolfgang's) are one puzzle: letters could go astray, particularly when they had to cross several borders, but four gone astray would be a lot – if that is the right number.[2] Another is the virtual blank during the seventeen days Mozart, by his own account, spent at Potsdam; lack of evidence proves nothing, but it leaves a question mark. His reason for then doubling back to Leipzig is likewise unclear. It may have been innocuous; the suggestion that it was an affair with Josepha Duschek (who, as Mozart himself told Constanze, was in Leipzig during his second visit) remains just that – a suggestion that may or may not be true. Another, perhaps likelier suggestion is that the embarrassment noticeable in his last letter to Constanze from Berlin may have to do with money rather than sex: if he had lost money gambling, assurances – underlined – that 'I shan't make much money' were in order.

There seems no reason to doubt the genuineness of Mozart's love for Constanze as he expressed it in his letters – even if he was having an affair. 'Dearest little wife! I am simply aching for news of you.' 'Today is the sixth day since I left you and by heaven! it seems a year.' 'O Stru! Stri! I kiss and squeeze you 1095060437082 times (now you can practise your pronunciation) . . .'

Soon after he returned to Vienna Constanze fell ill. Nothing is known about her health until then, and little about Mozart's. According to Leopold, he suffered in 1784 an attack of the rheumatic fever he had had as a child (though it took the form of 'colic'), and his doctor noted another, unspecified illness in 1787; Mozart himself reported having been ill in June–July 1789 after his return from Berlin, and complained now and then of headache and toothache. Constanze's illness was more severe. She was treated with leeches, a standard remedy, felt somewhat better, but then got bedsores. Mozart wrote to Puchberg in July: 'the only fear is that the bone may be affected. She is extraordinarily resigned and awaits recovery or death with true philosophic calm.' She then recovered enough to take the cure her doctor advised at Baden, a spa near Vienna.

Constanze's illness remains mysterious. After having given birth to four children in five years she was again five months pregnant. It would not be remarkable if she had a circulatory illness of some kind; there is a later reference to trouble with her foot. Mozart's talk of danger to the bone and of 'recovery or death' may show that she had an infection and the doctor feared gangrene, a common hazard at the time. All was well in the end, but meanwhile she spent months at Baden – from August until sometime in autumn 1789, from June to September 1790, in June–July 1791 (when she was again pregnant), and, briefly, in October 1791. That meant extra expense. Mozart visited her from time to time; back in Vienna, he worried about her getting into disreputable company – in 1789, about her being too free and easy with male visitors.

The purpose of the 1790 trip to Frankfurt was to be on hand during the coronation festivities. Mozart was uninvited, but so were many others. 'I am firmly resolved', he told Constanze, 'to make as much money as I can here and then return to you with great joy. What a glorious life we shall have then! I will work – work so hard – that no unforeseen accidents shall ever reduce us to such desperate straits again.' Two days later he was already warning Constanze that the money would be 'certainly not as much as you and some of my friends expect'. Sure enough, his concert in the big Frankfurt theatre – he played two concertos and a fantasy, interspersed with arias – was 'a splendid success from the point of view of honour and glory, but a failure as far as money was concerned'; there is independent witness that 'not very many people' attended, perhaps because too much was going on elsewhere.

A performance at Mainz before the Elector of that state likewise brought, as Wolfgang reported, a 'meagre sum' – the equivalent of 165 florins. Performances of *Seraglio* in Frankfurt and *Figaro* at Mannheim – he helped at rehearsals – offset a *Don Giovanni* cancelled, for unknown reasons, at Frankfurt; neither paid him anything. In Munich the Elector Karl Theodor no doubt rewarded him for taking part in a concert for the visiting king and queen of Naples (the new emperor's sister and brother-in-law, who had earlier been in Vienna); 'it is greatly to the credit of the Viennese Court', Mozart commented, 'that the king has to hear me in a foreign country'. Financially the tour was another setback.

'To me everything is cold – cold as ice', he had written to Constanze from Frankfurt two days after his arrival. 'Perhaps if you were with me I might possibly take more pleasure in the kindness of those I meet here. But, as it is, everything seems empty.'

This needs to be put in context. The moment he heard from Constanze three days later, 'at last I feel comforted and happy.' From Mainz he improvised a fantasy: he had been weeping over the paper, but now 'catch! – An astonishing number of kisses are flying about – The deuce! – I see a whole crowd of them! Ha! Ha! . . . I have just caught three – They are delicious!' 'Cold as ice' seems at first glance hardly more than a loving husband's reaction to being out of touch, stated in terms of eighteenth-century 'sensibility'.

How we interpret it matters: a school of thought, now out of fashion (but not necessarily wrong), sees in the works of Mozart's last phase a 'farewell to life' or at least a sense of unearthly detachment. Others find a change of style: an attempt to meet the fashion for simplicity, or a move towards neo-classicism.

Again, we might think 'cold as ice', 'everything seems empty' a token of deep depression. As a twenty-two-year-old faced with initial disappointment in Paris – but before his mother's death – Wolfgang had written 'I often wonder whether life is worth living.' Such moods come to many of us, and probably always have. It does not follow either from this or from his tragic compositions of the late 1780s that

Mozart was clinically depressive; nor do his bursts of high spirits suggest a manic-depressive.

His brother-in-law the actor-painter Joseph Lange, author of an eager, slightly flattering portrait, recalled in his memoirs that when working flat out Mozart would speak 'confusedly and disconnectedly', would sometimes make obscene jokes, and 'even deliberately forgot himself in his behaviour'. That sounds like the Mozart of the early letters, blowing off steam in the excitement of creation; in his last year he still wrote nonsense words to Constanze (he was her 'Knaller Praller Schnip-Schnap-Schnur') and faked a burlesque letter from his assistant, signed 'Franz Süssmayr, Muckshitter' (their handwriting was much alike; after Mozart's death Süssmayr was to return the compliment by faking, in all seriousness, the latter part of the Requiem). Lack of custom rather than deep depression, on the face of it, accounts for the very few works Mozart completed in 1790.

Near the end of that year, however, the tide began to turn. A private patron, a violinist who had married a rich wife, commissioned two string quintets (K. 593 and 614) – works written for a knowledgeable client, less impassioned than the two great 1787 quintets. Even a piano concerto turned out once again to be feasible; Mozart completed it in January and played it on 5 March 1791 at a concert run by another musician in Himmelpfortgasse ('Gate of Heaven Lane') – his last appearance in Vienna as soloist. This, he tacitly acknowledged, was a one-off: against his earlier practice, he sold the concerto for publication. Hanging on to manuscript music was worth while only if he saw a chance of again performing it himself.

This concerto in B♭ (K. 595) is a touchstone of Mozart's 'late style'. (True, some of it is on paper Mozart used in 1788; Alan Tyson, who thinks he began it in that year, argues that he is unlikely to have reached for some old paper in a bottom drawer, because that was not his practice as we can observe it. Few of us, surely, are so very predictable in our habits; the question remains open. If Tyson is right, the beginnings of the 'late style' should perhaps be dated from 1788, just before the near-hiatus of the bad years 1789–90.)

'Every stirring of energy is rejected or suppressed', Alfred Einstein wrote – arguing that the concerto showed Mozart resigned 'at the gate of eternity' – 'and this fact makes all the more uncanny the depths of sadness that are touched in the shadings and modulations of the harmony.' The finale with its leaping, folk-song-like initial theme had 'a veiled joyfulness, as if blessed children were playing in Elysian fields, joyful, but without hate and without love'. The work as a whole showed the 'second naiveté' of an artist who had got through complexity and out to the far side.

Einstein may have overdone it – the pianist has a chance to be force-ful, at least in Mozart's own cadenzas – but the first modulation near the end of the opening orchestral statement indeed has about it an infinite yet detached mercy; in that first Allegro quiet sighs attend the piano's slipping into the minor; the extraordinary series of key changes that lead to the recapitulation work through a pallid to an uncanny and, last, to a universal sadness, yet the music never raises a cry, never goes beyond self-communion. Slow footsteps in the Larghetto recur, once with the piano nakedly alone, elsewhere flanked by reticent chordal interjections or a falling phrase that does seem to say goodbye. In the final Allegro others besides Einstein have heard children whose rollicking is not of this earth, warned, near the end, by a series of more and more jarring chords – as, at that very time, the 'Nurse's Song' warned them in lines Blake was engraving for *Songs of Experience*:

> Then come home, my children, the sun is gone down,
> And the dews of night arise;
> Your spring & your day are wasted in play,
> And your winter and night in disguise.

As the *Songs of Innocence* balanced this with a parallel 'Nurse's song' ('The little ones leaped & shouted & laugh'd And all the hills ecchoèd'), so the B♭ concerto ends in quick bright impressions and a cheerful flourish. Written for closest interplay between soloist and orchestra rather than for brilliance, it is far removed from the grandeur of the C major (K. 503), the last of the royal Vienna series: the conqueror now meditates alone, apart.

A sense of detachment runs through the other main instrumental work Mozart wrote in his final year, the clarinet concerto in A (K. 622); this too he may have begun earlier, perhaps in 1789. Originally for a kind of basset horn, it was meant for his friend and fellow Mason Anton Stadler to perform, as he did in Prague that October.

What seems not of this earth is the concerto's withdrawal from the passions that agitate men and women. Not even the 'uncanny' filtering clouds of the piano concerto run across its serenity. A conductor can nudge it towards wanness, but even that goes no further than the transparency of a life self-consumed; Mahler's 'farewell' last movements in *Das Lied von der Erde* and the Ninth Symphony are, by comparison, memory-laden. In the play of soloist and orchestra, so knitted together as to rule out a cadenza, Mozart's writing attains a perfection that seeks no notice: the astonishing modulations, the varied wind harmony of the 'royal' piano concertos and the late symphonies give way to accompaniments so finely calibrated as to make a sound at once enchanting and diaphanous. We might call this the draining of Eros from Mozart's creative personality.

Not that he withdrew from Eros in his daily life. The change was rather a loss in his music of iridescent feeling and outward-going drive. If it was a move towards neo-classicism, the closest parallel may be Canova's sculpture at its best, the nude refined and smoothed to make an almost abstract statement. There was nothing abstract in these last months about Mozart's feeling for his wife:

> I am delighted that you have a good appetite [he wrote to her at Baden on 6 June] – but whoever gorges a lot, must also shit a lot – no, walk a lot, I mean. But I should not like you to take long *walks* without me. I entreat you to follow my advice exactly, for it comes from the heart. Adieu – my love – my only one. Do catch them in the air – those 2999½ little kisses from me which are flying about, waiting for someone to snap them up. Listen, I want to whisper something in your ear – and you in mine – and now we open and close our mouths again – again

and again – at last we say: 'It is all about Plumpi – Strumpi –' Well, you can think what you like – that is just why it's so convenient. Adieu. A thousand tender kisses.

As this suggests, by the spring of 1791 Mozart was outwardly more cheerful. Though he seems still to have been borrowing money, he had work in hand, as well as other means of earning and so of gradually cutting down the debt. The B♭ piano concerto was one of many publications that year: extrapolating from what the same publisher paid Haydn, H. C. Robbins Landon has calculated that between printed music and manuscript copies Mozart may have earned over 700 florins, almost equal to his salary. Much of this was dance music. Mozart apparently scribbled on a receipt for some of it 'Too much for what I did, not enough for what I could do.' If the source is accurate (Constanze's second husband, who read papers now lost) here again is the modern self-conscious artist, no longer content with the journalistic routine he had to keep up.

Mozart had prospects as well. The composer-organist of St Stephen's Cathedral, Leopold Hofmann, seemed to be mortally ill, but then recovered somewhat. Mozart applied to the patrons, the Vienna city council, for the reversion of the post – that is, he would succeed Hofmann at his death and would meanwhile act as unpaid assistant; on 28 April the council agreed. In the event, Hofmann was to outlive him.

'My musical talents', Mozart wrote in his application, 'my works, and my skill in composition are well known in foreign countries, my name is treated everywhere with some respect, and I myself have the honour to be employed as composer to the Court of Vienna...' He was 'peculiarly fitted' for the post 'on account of my thorough knowledge of both the secular and the ecclesiastical styles of music'. This was true, but so far it had not helped much. The new factor was Leopold II, who was clearly going to allow greater freedom in church music – part of his endeavour to keep up the reforming impulse in church and state without alienating as many groups as his brother had. Mozart, composer of a line of sacred works still more innovative than Haydn's late masses and *Creation*, is another might-have-been.

Opera, though, remained the most important genre. In September 1791 Mozart had not one but two new operas performed. On the 6th *La Clemenza di Tito* opened in Prague – the gala opera presented by the Estates (governing body) of the Habsburg-ruled kingdom of Bohemia to Leopold II, who that morning had been crowned in the cathedral. On the 30th *The Magic Flute* opened in Vienna at the Theater an der Wieden, a suburban house run by Emanuel Schikaneder; he had written the libretto and sang the leading comic part of Papageno.

Neither came of a rise in Mozart's standing at court. The emperor (and, just as important, the empress) still preferred the Italian masters of 'pure' vocal writing, Cimarosa and Paisiello; these were not, for the moment, available. The Italian whom Leopold had inherited as court composer – Antonio Salieri, an able musician – had earlier had first refusal of *Così fan tutte*. The Prague impresario, Domenico Guardasoni, had been asked at two months' notice to supply a coronation opera; he now offered Salieri a contract to write it, but Salieri was too busy in Vienna. Once again Mozart was the second choice. The goodwill he had earned in Prague with *Figaro* and *Don Giovanni* probably led the aristocratic group of officials (without whose leave Guardasoni would not have acted) to fall back on him – even though some knew the court to be prejudiced against his music. Local feeling may have come into it: Prague would show Vienna a thing or two.

Schikaneder's theatre had nothing to do with the court. Though far from the shack sometimes alleged – it was a well-appointed house holding about a thousand – it drew a mixed audience, some of them shopkeepers and artisans, who came to marvel at transformation scenes and laugh at the misadventures of traditional Viennese clown figures. Mozart had known Schikaneder since the actor-manager and his troupe had played Salzburg in 1780; he had written the odd aria for them, and must have heard them perform *Seraglio* in Vienna in 1784. With his love of theatregoing he had no doubt seen many of the productions Schikaneder had put on since taking over the Theater an der

Wieden in 1789, in some of which Constanze's sister Josepha Hofer appeared; the two men were fellow Masons besides.

Mozart, it seems, agreed to write *The Magic Flute* sometime in the early spring of 1791, concentrated on it in May and June, and had much of it written by mid-July, when Guardasoni sidetracked him onto the Prague coronation opera.

What lay behind it? Did it embody a sustained attempt to justify Freemasonry at a time when the brotherhood was under threat – or was it a routine commercial enterprise, tinged with Masonic allegory and lifted onto a higher plane by Mozart?

We have only indirect evidence to go on – that of the work itself, but also that of Schikaneder's other works and the contemporary Viennese theatre as a whole. Schikaneder's biographer Kurt Honolka, one of the few people to go through the huge output of those years, has shown that *The Magic Flute* was, from one point of view, a compendium of theatrical clichés. Of the features we now meet there and scarcely anywhere else in opera – oriental wise men, Masonic allusions, human qualities prized above hierarchical status, parallel noble and plebeian couples, ordeals, magical transformations, flaming helmets, birdcatchers, birdmen – some were knocking about the attics of the European mind; rather more furnished the Viennese commercial stage.

The many literary origins scholars have proposed no doubt played a part. Schikaneder, however, needed to do little beyond reshaping material he knew to have worked well in some theatrical entertainment. The outcome depended a good deal on Mozart, who seems to have influenced, perhaps cajoled Schikaneder into writing a libretto a cut above his usual standard. The opera's total gesture needs to be examined on its own. Meanwhile it seems unlikely that composer and librettist set out to rescue Freemasonry in Vienna from a doom that did not strike it until nearly three years later. In the spring and early summer of 1791 the French Revolution was still in its moderate constitutional phase; members of the Viennese governing class might be anxious about such things as the abolition of titles, but the events that were to panic them – democracy, war, massacre, regicide – lay a year or so ahead.

Once Mozart got the contract for the Prague coronation opera he needed to work fast, but not – as used to be thought – over a mere eighteen days. Time was indeed short: Guardasoni fell back, as he was allowed to, on a 1734 libretto that had served about forty composers. *La clemenza di Tito* was suitable because in it the Vienna court poet Metastasio had implied praise for the magnanimity of Leopold II's grandfather. Its long recitatives and string of arias were, however, out of date; Caterino Mazzolà, briefly the holder of Metastasio's post, did a rush job of turning it into what Mozart called a 'true opera'. This meant bringing in the kind of numbers Italian librettists now resorted to in serious opera: duets, trios, choruses, and, as in comic opera, a first-half finale that assembled most of the characters on stage for a highly dramatic confrontation.

As Mozart started work Constanze gave birth on 26 July to their last – and second surviving – child. The impresario had gone on to Italy to sign up a leading castrato and prima donna. Until he came back with news of their vocal range – something the composer had to know before he could fit their parts to them – Mozart could work only on ensembles and on arias for the tenor, whose voice he was familiar with, though he bent the rules by adapting as the heroine's big final aria one he had already written for Josepha Duschek. When Guardasoni came back sometime in August Mozart was able to get on with the rest and, no doubt, send some music ahead.

Probably on 25 August, he, Constanze, and Süssmayr left for Prague; as on the 1783 trip to Salzburg, they left behind a one-month-old child, who this time came to no harm. Much of *Tito* – Alan Tyson has shown from watermarks – was already written; in the nine days Mozart had in Prague before the first night he still had to write – and the company had to learn – an aria, a march, the overture, and two accompanied recitatives. He had, it seems, farmed out the 'plain' recitatives (accompanied by continuo only) to Süssmayr – not an unusual step when time pressed.

Altogether Mozart wrote *La clemenza di Tito* in seven to eight weeks. The exact time depended on how soon Mazzolà could let him have part of the libretto; it included the three-and-a-half-day coach trip through the hot, golden countryside of Lower Austria and Bohemia, when he could compose in his head. This schedule was not in itself uncommon, though it was unusual for the composer not to know right away who would be singing the leads, and for the company to learn as much as they probably had to in the last few days of rehearsal. For Mozart the task was a lucky chance: it paid 900 florins, twice as much as an ordinary opera, and offered a return match after the disappointment of the Frankfurt coronation.

The opening night was, however, a near-failure. The empress may or may not have called *Tito* 'una porcheria tedesca' ('German rubbish'); she certainly wrote 'the opera was not much and the music very bad, so that almost all of us fell asleep'. The nobleman who had thought *Così fan tutte* 'charming' found *Tito* 'most boring'. The audience were probably tired from the morning's coronation ritual, and the singers from last-minute rehearsals. Later performances were ill attended but for the last; as Mozart, back in Vienna, was delighted to hear, it brought 'tremendous applause'.

'Exquisite grace and rarely redeemed dullness': Charles Rosen's verdict on *Tito* nearly thirty years ago is now out of fashion; the thing to say is that the work is every bit as fine as the other major operas. Audiences may secretly share his feeling.

The libretto is part of the trouble. Italian serious opera as a showcase for a castrato and a prima donna was a dying form, however titivated. Metastasio's dramas were, in their way, cogent; pulling them about obscured their mathematical logic and deft psychology (A loves B who loves C, with permutations) but made them no more gripping to audiences who, like us, were reading novels and looking for character and high colour. Mozart's response suggests that, even as a 'true opera', *Tito* fired his imagination only here and there. Elsewhere we seem to hear the composer turning out music to a high standard, but deliberately rather than spontaneously engaged.

Neither the occasion nor the stage he had reached in his artistic and personal development allowed anything as outward-going or innovative as Idomeneo. In Tito, Mozart keeps many of the numbers short; even when he spreads himself in the big arias for the leads he orchestrates sparingly, with obbligato solos (for Anton Stadler on clarinet or basset horn) in only two. At times he writes in the style of comic opera, even German comic opera, as in the duet for two sopranos 'Ah perdona al primo affetto' – little more than an exquisitely simple melody repeated three times, appropriate for lovers united in sorrow – or in the duettino for the hero and his friend, which takes less than ninety seconds. Fine as these numbers are, they sit uneasily to the elaborate arias that follow. Così fan tutte had contrasting short and long numbers, but no such contrast of style unless as a deliberate parody; serious and comic opera were drawing closer together, a fusion Tito exemplified better in its trios than in these stylistically ill-matched numbers.

Much in the work is grand: the marches, the long arias, above all the Act I finale, when fire breaks out in the Capitol and the chorus wails out of sight, then draws closer as five principals join in spare, dramatic exchanges. Grand, by and large impersonal – a blend of qualities found in much neo-classical art; this helps to explain why Tito became the favourite Mozart opera of the years 1800–20, and fell away as Romanticism took hold. Music can seem drained of personal feeling yet intense and memorable, like the Clarinet Concerto. La clemenza di Tito is by any reckoning a distinguished work; how much of it lives in the minds of the audience after curtain fall?

No such question need be asked about The Magic Flute. It was an immediate success, had 20 performances in its first month, 198 in its first two years, and has never looked back.

Most modern opera houses are too big for the spoken dialogue, which easily falls flat; Mozart himself remarked 'you have no idea how charming the music sounds when you hear it … close to the orchestra' – and that was in a theatre of a size we keep for plays. Conductors, besides, often take it too slowly; scene changes destroy tension if they are not immediate, as in an eighteenth-century theatre. Yet it seldom fails to leave the audience with a sense of having been healed. In this they are probably at one with the Viennese who filled the theatre night after night: 'what always gives me most pleasure', Mozart told Constanze about a week into the run, 'is the *silent approval*! You can see how this opera is becoming more and more esteemed.' Antonio Salieri, an early attender and in some sense a rival, freely admired what he called an *operone*, a great opera.

'Novel and delicious' – so a visiting Englishman summed up the kind of entertainment the opera stood for: 'founded upon the fictions of imagination, it sets probability at defiance, and justifies the wildest caprice of genius'. The libretto, for many years dismissed as cheap and absurd, is once again in favour. We now think of myth as rooted in the unconscious; it can hold together feelings and kinds of behaviour that seem contradictory because those contradictions are inherent in the basic experiences of men and women. Ingmar Bergman's film of *The Magic Flute* could make the bad-good and good-bad figures, Sarastro and the Queen of Night, into Pamina's estranged parents and make sense, not because that was what Schikaneder and Mozart intended but because the fable they devised had the resonance – arbitrary, ambiguous, by turns bewildering and delightful – of what a child experiences as it grows up.

The authors scarcely had time to theorise; that may be why they could bring off an archetypal work. When Mozart got back from Prague, perhaps little more than ten days before the first night, he still had to write the priests' march, the boys' trio in Act 2, Pamina's aria, and her trio with Tamino and Sarastro as well as the overture. Both he and the company were used to working fast; we need not put down the 'inconsistencies' to hurry.

Mozart – if we assume him to have had a considerable share in the libretto – probably cared a good deal more about the effect in the theatre than about the explanations scholars have found for the 'inconsistencies', reasoned though they may be. To the audience the drift of the story has always been clear: a young prince finds enlightenment in those who had earlier seemed hateful; the young woman he loves overcomes fears and dangers, and her mother's influence, to be with him; an ordinary man settles for the pleasures of food, drink, and married life. That the queen, a wronged woman, is an evil, vengeful figure, that the wise leader Sarastro keeps the villainous Monostatos as a servant and then orders a cruel punishment for him (remitted – as we may or may not gather from an inconspicuous line, often cut), that Pamina somehow gets back the dagger that was taken from her – these are the ways of fable. The characters, too, may go against their earlier behaviour when they face the audience and moralise: the three ladies preach the discretion they have just done their best to undermine.

The most famous 'inconsistency' raises the question of what Mozart and Schikaneder had in mind when they brought in a lightly veiled Masonic order from which women are excluded. The wise priests twice warn Tamino against women's chatter and cunning, Sarastro tells Pamina 'a man must guide your hearts', yet at the end her courage in facing night and death at her lover's side entitles her to become a wise priest herself. Mozart believed in, perhaps demanded this ending: so we may assume after hearing the music he wrote for Pamina, not just the aria of grief 'Ach, ich fühl's' but her great cry for the truth at all costs and her confession to Sarastro: the music of young heroism.

Freemasonry's part in the work is notable but not all-pervading. Masonic musical symbolism comes in with the opening chords, yet it is far from consistently applied. Masonic ideas become explicit when the priests gather to vote on Tamino's admission to the order – a solemn moment, deliberately left as speech punctuated by the three-fold Masonic chords. The crucial exchange now seems quaint. Tamino, a priest implies, may not come through the ordeals: 'he is a prince!' 'Better still', Sarastro replies, 'he is a human being!' In 1791 it was hardly revolutionary – Joseph II had implied as much – but, in a still hierarchical society, it needed saying. Monostatos ('single state') lampooned the monastic orders, the target of Masonic as of much

17 The Theater an der Wieden in the year of *The Magic Flute*: from a contemporary
    almanac. This view suggests the closeness of some of the audience to the stage,
    hence the intimacy with which Schikaneder as Papageno could address them.

other criticism; his blackness implied the cowl rather than Africa. Suitably, he joined up with the queen, symbol of a reaction against 'enlightened' thought that did not have to be pinned down to a single person or institution.

The burden of the work – we may call it ideological or religious – comes at us in the music, more precisely in five kinds of music.

There is, first, the solemn music of the priests' marches, their two invocations to Isis and Osiris, and Sarastro's aria extolling friendship and forgiveness, 'In diesen heil'gen Hallen'. Mildness and majesty soar in unexampled union above a harmony solemn with dark instruments – bassoon and horn, at times basset-horn and trombone – whose texture is at once rich and light. Sarastro's music, according to Shaw, was the only one fit for the mouth of God, but that misses the point. There is in it neither the apprehension of an unknown power nor the joy in resurrection that mark Christian faith; the power is known, and – whatever the calls on Isis and Osiris, pale deities – it is a human power; we may rejoice, but in human wisdom. Even the church music borrowed by the men in armour as they tell the young prince about the ordeals – a Lutheran chorale above a four-part fugato – manages to be solemn without transcendence. It is a token of Mozart's insight that exaltation of the human never grows complacent or overbearing. *The Magic Flute* is an unrepeatable climax of 'enlightened' faith in human beings' ability to guide themselves and the world; while it lasts, it rings true.

When the men in armour finish their solemn warning they go off into a comic opera allegretto, making, in Erik Smith's words, an 'incongruous but delightful mixture of the supernatural with the informal'. This is the second kind of music, where the supernatural indeed glimmers, but in the accents of fairy tale: the boys' trios, lightly scored for a few winds and strings, pizzicato or fluttering; the enchantments of flute and glockenspiel; even the extraordinary, spare music that takes Pamina and Tamino through the ordeals by fire and water – flute over hushed brass and drum, at once ethereal and of deep import. It is 'music i' th' air, under the earth'; magic; 'the fictions of imagination' at their most taking.

The third kind of music informs certain crucial passages: the confrontation between Tamino and the old priest outside the temple; the duet for Pamina and Sarastro; the trio for those two and Tamino; and the scene between Pamina and Tamino – later joined by the men in armour – where she undertakes to go with him through the ordeals, protected by the flute her father carved from the heart of the thousand-year-old oak (her G minor aria is a jewel off the same chain). In all these scenes the characters – Sarastro included – grow in insight; nobility is the tone, a highly innovative freedom of musical writing the means, with recitative, arioso, and fragments of more patterned melody carrying the inner action forward and little or no repetition. Technically this music points towards Weber's *Euryanthe*, hence towards early Wagner; spiritually it does most to convince us of the dignity of human beings.

Of the last two kinds of music, one is the the stagiest, the other the closest to folk song. The Queen of Night's appearances combine fiery declamation with bursts of coloratura apt for a villainess galactically enthroned. What Papageno and, at the end, the Papagena of his heart's desire sing is the popular music of genius. Its inspired simplicity gives further evidence that human beings are worth while.

These different kinds of music – here is the astonishing thing – work together and do not jar. Not only does the logic of myth override differences; Mozart unified the score, as he failed to unify *La clemenza di Tito*, by musical means. All the patterned numbers are short by the standards of his earlier operas; the longest, those involving the three ladies, have plenty going on in them to justify the length, and in any case the writing throughout is succinct, with little repetition of words or music. The orchestration too, at once delicious and economical, hardly shows off single instruments other than the two magical ones; Mozart of set purpose cut it down as he went along.

'Our story set to the music of the spheres' is Erik Smith's summing up of *The Magic Flute*. Really it is our story set to our music, heard by the ear of genius.

While he was hard at work on the opera in June, and visiting Constanze from time to time at Baden, Mozart wrote a three-minute motet for the Baden choirmaster. 'Ave, verum corpus' (K. 618) was to be sung on the important feast of Corpus Christi, when a procession – banned by Joseph II but restored by his successor – would once again go through the streets. It is a feast of the Host; six short lines of text call up the incarnation, the crucifixion, and the believer's hope of taking the last sacrament before death. Mozart's setting, however – for four voices, organ, and strings – flows through the hymn in gently shifting harmony, with one shadow on the way and no hint of supernatural drama, no pointing at anything beyond itself. It is perfect of its kind. Unbelievers sometimes choose to have it sung at their funeral: rightly, for – whatever he intended – here as in The Magic Flute Mozart created the sound for a human condition where, as the three boys sing, 'earth can be heaven and mortals like gods'.

7 Requiem

Mozart died while composing the Requiem – a mass for the dead and so, apparently, for himself. This would have made people talk even if his death had not coincided with the onset of Romanticism, a movement deeply interested in the arcane. Add the commissioning of the work by an unknown man and you have the makings of a legend. Tales of mystery surrounding the Requiem and Mozart's death went on until 1964, when new-found documents cleared most of them up.

In July 1791 a stranger – a lawyer – did commission the Requiem, for a fee that may have been as much as 585 or 675 florins: more than the standard fee for an opera, hence well worth having, especially as some of it was to be paid in advance. The only mystery was the name of the person the lawyer was acting for, who did not wish to be known – though as he was the landlord of Mozart's friend Puchberg the mystery was perhaps not too dense.

That a patron should be anonymous was, for that matter, unlikely to trouble Mozart. Constanze indirectly suggested as much when, after his death, she applied for a widow's pension (it had to be an act of grace: Mozart had failed to produce the birth certificate needed to get into the musicians' pension scheme). She made a point of saying that Mozart's last illness had come just as his fortunes were improving: 'shortly before his death' he had been promised an annual subscription of 1,000 florins from some – unnamed – Hungarian nobles, and another for a still larger sum from equally unnamed persons in

Amsterdam; in exchange 'he would have had to compose only a few works for the exclusive use of the subscribers'. We have no other evidence, but these arrangements were like those the young Wolfgang had made with a Bohemian noble, and had tried to set up with ten inhabitants of Munich.

Mozart probably did not know all of these Hungarian and Dutch patrons. His childhood visits to Bratislava and Amsterdam were a quarter-century past. The acquaintances made there had dimmed; they belonged to a time when artists depended on great personages. Now a jobbing composer like Mozart could work on straightforward commercial terms for the owner of a mechanical organ, or for a group of patrons, like the Amsterdammers, whom he was unlikely to meet. So long as the money came in, their identity mattered little. The Requiem commission was not very different.

It came from an eccentric music lover, Count Walsegg, who held chamber concerts and other entertainments at his castle south of Vienna, in many of which he took part as cellist, flautist, or actor; he had lost his young wife in February 1791 and wished to commemorate her with a requiem mass. His quirk was a habit of commissioning scores from leading musicians, copying them out himself, and passing them off as his own work; not that he fooled the musicians in his employ. In 1793 he was to have the Requiem performed for his wife, still unaware that he in turn had been fooled: Mozart had lived to compose only some of it. The rest was Süssmayr's work; he had helped Constanze in a tight spot by faking Mozart's hand and signature. (When publication of the Requiem in 1800 showed the author to have been Mozart, not Walsegg, the count thought of taking 'serious measures' but appears to have let Constanze off with an apology in private.)

When Mozart got the commission in July he told Walsegg's agent that he could not at once start work on the Requiem. With two operas on the stocks and within weeks of their first performance, he was badly overworked all through July, August, and September. A man who saw him in Prague towards the end of that time wrote (after his death, perhaps with hindsight) that he had looked ill, kept taking medicine, and showed understandable signs of nervous exhaustion; on saying goodbye to his friends as he and Constanze left for Vienna he burst into tears.

Even after the opening of *The Magic Flute*, back in Vienna on 30 September, Mozart had to orchestrate the Clarinet Concerto; he had nearly finished it by 7 October. Almost certainly he did not start composing the Requiem until after that date; six weeks then went by, interrupted by a day or so while he fetched Constanze from Baden, and a few more days while he was writing a cantata for a Masonic occasion, finished on 15 November and performed at Mozart's lodge on the 18th. About 20 November he was so ill as to take to his bed; he died a fortnight later, just before 1 a.m. on 5 December.

Mozart's fatal illness remains a puzzle. In our own time several physicians have published diagnoses – unfortunately at variance. The version now widely accepted is that he was killed by the long-term consequences of the rheumatic fever he suffered as a child; he had had further attacks as an adult, in 1784, perhaps in 1787, and, if his mention of 'rheumatic pains' in the head is a guide, in April and perhaps August 1790. A rival theory that he suffered from Henoch-Schönlein syndrome, a disease of the immune system leading in some cases to kidney failure and death, has lost ground. The words used by Mozart's own doctors are unhelpful: these leaders of the profession stated him to have died of 'acute miliary fever', then a catch-all term for an infection accompanied by a rash. In his last days he clearly suffered from oedema (dropsy) – swelling caused by water. This appears in certain kinds of heart disease, especially in the last stages; repeated attacks of rheumatic fever can damage the valves of the heart as well as open the way to infections.

The surprise is not that Mozart died young, in all likelihood through such repeated attacks: others died in the same way, sped by doctors' propensity to bleed the sick. What is puzzling is that for much of his life he remained active and, it seems, in tolerable health. Even in the first half of October 1791 his letters to Constanze at Baden were gossipy and cheerful, with no sign of illness or of his putting a good face on it. He wrote several times that his servant Primus ('Don Primus') had brought him half a capon, or 'a delicious slice of sturgeon . . . I have sent him off again to fetch some more if he can'; another time 'what do I see? What do I smell? Why, here is Don Primus with the cutlets! Che gusto! [What a delicious taste!]. Now I am eating to your health! It is just striking eleven. Perhaps you are already asleep? St! St! I won't wake you.'

The success of The Magic Flute gave him deep pleasure. He went several times – on 13 October with his mother-in-law and his seven-year-old son Karl, then at a boarding school just outside Vienna; Karl was 'absolutely delighted'. At an earlier performance Mozart had played a trick on Schikaneder:

> during Papageno's aria with the glockenspiel I went behind the scenes, as I felt a sort of impulse today to play it myself. Well, just for fun, at the point where Schikaneder has a pause, I played an arpeggio. He was startled, looked behind the wings, and saw me. When he had his next pause, I played no arpeggio. This time he stopped and refused to go on. I guessed what he was thinking and again played a chord. He then struck the glockenspiel and said 'Shut up'. Whereupon everyone laughed. I am inclined to think that this joke taught many in the audience that Papageno does not play the instrument himself.

Mozart found time to deal with Karl's schooling: the boarding establishment provided fresh air but little else. He discussed sending the boy to the Piarists (Scolopi), a teaching order who used advanced educational methods.

Constanze, when she got back from Baden on 16 October, began to worry about her husband's condition: as she recalled a few years later in statements to his early biographers, it was getting worse and making him depressed. On 'a fine autumn day' – it seems to have been 20 or 21 October – they drove out to the Prater, the big Vienna park. 'Mozart began to speak of death; he maintained that he was writing the Requiem for himself. As he said this, tears came into his eyes, and when she attempted to talk him out of those black thoughts, he answered: "No, no, I feel it too strongly, I won't last much longer: surely I have been poisoned! I can't free myself of these thoughts."' She then, on medical advice, stopped him from working on the Requiem for a time, but when the success of his Masonic cantata cheered him up she let him start again – not for long.

Mozart's talk of poison became known after his death and started rumours that have not quite faded away. The most persistent rumour was that the rival composer Antonio Salieri had poisoned him; Pushkin made it into a play, Rimsky-Korsakov into an opera, and a variation on it – Salieri not as poisoner but as the eternally envious mediocre artist – has had a huge audience in Peter Shaffer's play and film *Amadeus*.

There is nothing in it. All composers in Vienna were in a sense Mozart's rivals, but Salieri was the most successful of all: court composer, hence far better paid than Mozart, favoured by Joseph II, able in his tragi-comic, Franco-Italian opera *Axur* – a resounding success ever since its first performance in 1788 – to blend all the styles then in vogue. Nor was he a mediocre artist by the standards of his age or ours; nor, finally, does it appear to be true that in his last senile years he accused himself of complicity in Mozart's death: one more tale set off by Romantic fancy over a genius dying young.

Mozart had indeed talked of 'Salieri's plots' – in December 1789, when he was preparing *Così fan tutte*. He, like his father, was apt to think other composers were plotting against him; that was often true, but 'plots' meant jockeying for commissions and talking down each other's works.

Mozart's own reason for talking of poison is clear. Until the late nineteenth century, when medical science discovered the bacterial causes of infection, many illnesses were unexplained. Poison was sometimes thought to have killed an eminent man or woman who died of a rapid infection like peritonitis. Mozart too was trying to account for a sickness that had no obvious cause. Constanze plainly did not share her husband's belief; she took it as a symptom of his weakened and depressed state.

18 The house in Rauhensteingasse where Mozart died: watercolour by
J. Wohlmuth

After the conversation in the Prater, Mozart was still able for two or
three weeks to go on with the Requiem; at one point he, Constanze,
and Süssmayr sang part of it. Once in bed, there was little he could do.
His symptoms grew alarmingly fast. His arms and legs were swollen,
so much that within a short time he could hardly move.

The most persuasive account of his last days comes from his
youngest sister-in-law Sophie Weber, then unmarried and living with
her mother not far away. Her recollections date from thirty-four years
later, yet they are for the most part concrete and ring true; once or
twice she may have suppressed painful details. Constanze's account
to two early biographers, one of them her second husband, fills out
her sister's.

Because Mozart could no longer turn in bed the two sisters made
him a night-jacket which he could put on frontways. 'Then, as we
didn't know how seriously ill he was, we also made him a quilted
dressing-gown . . . so that when he got up he should have everything
he needed . . . he was really delighted with [it].' On some days he felt
better; once he told Sophie that he would go and congratulate her

mother on her name day; he seemed 'bright and happy'. At other times he was despondent at leaving his wife and children unprovided for just as his fortunes seemed to be looking up. On 4 December, after a night so dreadful that Constanze thought he might not be alive by morning, he had the score of the Requiem brought to him and looked it over: 'Didn't I say before that I was writing this Requiem for myself?'

That afternoon Sophie, at her mother's, had a presentiment – a candle went out – and rushed to the Mozarts'. She found Constanze 'almost despairing and yet trying to keep calm'. 'Do stay with me today', Constanze urged her, 'for if he has another bad turn he will pass away tonight. Go in to him for a little while and see how he is.'

> He immediately called me to him and said: 'Ah, dear Sophie, how glad I am that you have come. You must stay here tonight and see me die.' I tried hard to be brave and to persuade him to the contrary. But to all my attempts he only replied: 'Why, I already have the taste of death on my tongue.' And, 'if you do not stay, who will support my dearest Constanze?' 'Yes, yes, dear Mozart', I assured him, 'but first I must go back to our mother and tell her that you would like me to stay with you today. Otherwise she will think that some misfortune has befallen you.' 'Yes, do so', said Mozart, 'but be sure and come back soon.'

Constanze then begged her sister to fetch a priest and make it look like 'a chance call' – obviously so as not to let Mozart realise that he might indeed be at the point of death. With the greatest difficulty Sophie persuaded one to come; the trouble, apparently, was that Mozart had not himself asked for a priest and the 'chance call' would have about it a touch of deception. (The alternative explanation, that Mozart was known to be anticlerical, is less likely: anticlerical feeling was common; even if the priest had thought Mozart actively anti-Christian – which we have no reason to suppose – he would still allow for the possibility of repentance.) The priest – if we assume him to have come while Sophie was at her mother's; even this is not clear – administered extreme unction, but not the Eucharist.

When Sophie got back from her mother's she found Mozart urging his wife to keep his death a secret until she could inform J. G. Albrechtsberger, the court organist, and give him time to apply for Mozart's assistantship at St Stephen's Cathedral (he got the job). Constanze had a search made for Mozart's doctor; he was found at the theatre but 'had to wait' for the end of the play. When he came he ordered cold poultices to be placed on Mozart's burning head; these gave him a shock. Probably at this point, Mozart vomited – in a brown arc – and became unconscious. Constanze, Sophie, and the doctor kept watch. Mozart died about two hours later, in Sophie's arms: his last movement she understood as 'an attempt to express with his mouth the drum passages in the Requiem. That I can still hear.'

Constanze, by her own account, 'crawled into the bed of her dead husband, to catch his illness and to die with him'; Sophie recalled that her sister 'in her utter misery threw herself on her knees and implored the Almighty for his aid. She simply could not tear herself away from Mozart . . .' After daylight broke the news spread, the house filled up with grieving friends, and people could be heard weeping in the street outside.

Baron van Swieten came and set about arranging Mozart's funeral. Leopold II had dismissed him that very day from his post as head of the board of education – part of the new emperor's cautious retreat from his brother's more radical plans. Van Swieten, however, still held to Joseph II's austere view of ritual and in particular of funerals, which until the late emperor's reforms had often been lavish. It was probably on his advice, and not just because money was short, that Constanze paid for the cheapest of the three classes of funeral Joseph's reforms had set up. (We know nothing about any wishes Mozart may have expressed.) Technically it was not the pauper's funeral so often mentioned, but it was no more elaborate.

On 6 December, a calm, unusually mild day, the coffin was taken to St Stephen's Cathedral for the funeral service, and, that night, to the burial ground of St Marx some three miles out. We do not know who attended the service; Constanze was too unwell to go. We do know that no one went to the burial ground other than the attendants. There the body, taken out of the reusable coffin and wrapped in a linen sack, was sprinkled with quicklime and laid in a grave with four or five others. Within seven years such graves were emptied and reused. Because of this, no one knows just where Mozart was buried or where his remains might be.

All this was a matter of imperial regulation – soon afterwards given up: Joseph II's austere measures went too flatly against the human wish to keep some visible token of the dead. While they lasted, they were observed: Mozart's funeral was like that of most of his Viennese contemporaries. Tales of his being buried as a pauper, in a snow-storm, are part of the romantic legend.

Constanze and her children, however, risked becoming paupers. Her first task was to raise some money and cope with the debts. She successfully petitioned the emperor for an ex gratia widow's pension (of one-third Mozart's salary – 267 florins a year), arranged concerts, and sold music to copyists, publishers, and the King of Prussia. Within a few months she and her family were in the clear; within a few years she consolidated Mozart's reputation by selling many of his works to leading German publishing houses. The activity probably helped her through the worst of the period of mourning.

Right after Mozart's death one of her chief concerns was to collect the fee for the Requiem and not have to pay back the advance. This meant delivering as complete a score of which Mozart had written only a part.

He had composed in short score (voices, figured bass, and some frag-ments of instrumental parts) the Introitus, the Dies irae sequence (all but the latter part of the Lacrymosa), and the Offertorium, but had orches-trated only the Introitus. The Sanctus, Benedictus, Agnus Dei, and Lux aeterna were yet to be written. People close to Mozart – not only Constanze but others who wished to support her story – made out that he had discussed these latter numbers with his assistant Süssmayr or had sketched out ideas for them. Nothing, however, has survived other than a sketched beginning of an Amen fugue to end the Dies irae sequence.

19 Canova, tomb of the Archduchess Christina in the Augustinian Church, Vienna. This work, conceived four years after Mozart's death, embodied the neo-classical aesthetic that informs the Requiem and some other late Mozart works – at once poignant and austere.

The simplest interpretation is that the latter part of the Requiem as we have it is by Süssmayr; the work as a whole ought to be known as 'by Mozart and Süssmayr', just as *Henry VIII* should be labelled 'by Shakespeare and Fletcher'. Constanze did not at first entrust the Requiem to Süssmayr, because – she later explained – she was annoyed with him; the reason was probably that he had been making up to Salieri. She therefore first asked a former pupil of her husband's, Joseph Eybler, to finish the work. With help from another composer, F. J. Freystädtler, he completed some of the orchestration, but gave up. She then turned to Süssmayr, who finished the job.

We had best not see Mozart out of life with this hybrid work. His share in it is more fragmentary than the incomplete Mass in C minor. Parts of the Requiem are merely decorous – and they are not all Süssmayr's: the trombone solo at the Tuba mirum (the annunciation of the last trump), with its upward sequence that strains after majesty and fails, is Mozart's. True, the fugal Kyrie and the Dies irae have a driving power, the Recordare for the soloists is wonderfully limpid and expectant, and the Lacrymosa's sighing figure – in its first eight bars, as far as Mozart took it – encapsulates mourning. The opening with its dark orchestration ruled by basset horn and bassoon is stern, even peremptory at the words 'rest eternal give them, Lord' – as Haydn in his Paukenmesse a few years later was to beat the drum and demand fiercely 'give us peace'; both men spoke, it may be, to the time of prolonged European crisis and war that was breaking out at Mozart's death.

Mozart is best seen off with his last completed work of real significance, *The Magic Flute*. Its deep humanity is still with us; so is the promise it holds out of felicity through human wisdom, though two more centuries of human behaviour witness against it. Or, best of all, with the 'Ave, verum corpus' he composed while working on the opera. Perfection attained through the most economical of means; all outward signs gone of the tension, the anxiety, the heights and depths of feeling that speak to us in many of his other works, yet those heights and depths not turned back from but gathered into solace through the power of music: here is a fitting memorial. Mozart's voice still gives a sound we inwardly recognise: of all composers in the European tradition, he is our man.

4 Man of the theatre

1 Rosen, writing in 1970, saw this happening in *The Marriage of Figaro* and later operas; he thought that in *Idomeneo* Mozart sometimes inexplicably failed to master 'a large rhythmic movement over a long stretch of time': *The Classical Style* (London, 1971), pp. 167, 175–6, 180. Experience of performances since then might have changed his mind.

2 According to her highly dramatic narrative, Anna was in her 'rooms' when the seducer arrived, she at first mistaking him for Ottavio: that is, she was not in a bedroom but in the then usual suite of corridorless, multi-purpose rooms, her part of the family palace, and she happened to be alone; there would have been nothing unusual in a gentleman's dropping in late at night, for aristocrats got up late and went to bed late. Her music, besides, tells of her clarion outrage at Don Giovanni's attack – no hint that it succeeded – and her heartfelt love for Ottavio; it nowhere suggests that she is lying. The year's wait she requests before she marries Ottavio (a mere twenty-four hours have gone by since her father's death) is what was then thought seemly.

5 Mozart and God

1 The quintet is paired with that in C, completed by 19 April. Mozart worked on both at once, as Alan Tyson has shown from the paper used for the C major and for the discarded opening of a finale to the

G minor; he then switched to different paper for the final version of K. 516. News of Leopold's illness had reached him on 4 April. Complex chamber works, as we know from the string quartets, gave him a great deal of trouble and could take him months or even years: it seems virtually inconceivable that he could have written both the C major quintet and a first version of the G minor in a fortnight. Both must have been on the stocks before 4 April.

6 The last phase

1 In writing to his wife from Frankfurt on 8 October 1790, Mozart talked of a prospective 2,000-florin loan (involving Hoffmeister in some way) from which 20 per cent interest would be deducted at the start, leaving 1,600 florins. It is unclear (a) whether the loan was actually made on these terms when he returned to Vienna and (b) how many years' interest the 400 florins deducted would have represented (Maynard Solomon's assumption that this was the two-year loan from Lackenbacher – which in any case was for 1,000 florins – is unproven). No conclusions can therefore be drawn as to the annual rate of interest Mozart was prepared to pay. He had earlier told Puchberg that he did not care how much he would have to repay, but that was probably a rhetorical flourish.

2 That four letters listed by Mozart as having been sent are now missing does not prove that they were all lost at the time. Constanze complained of not having heard from him for some time – that is all we know. Mozart was in any event slapdash in reckoning intervals between dates and perhaps in listing the letters themselves.

What follows is a choice of reading available in English. Readers wanting more should consult the bibliographies in The New Grove or in Maynard Solomon's life, listed below.

The fundamental sources for Mozart's life are The Letters of Mozart and his Family, translated by Emily Anderson (3rd revised edn, London, 1985), and the other contemporary documents gathered in O. E. Deutsch, ed., Mozart: A Documentary Biography (London, 1965), supplemented by C. Eisen, ed., New Mozart Documents (London, 1991).

A remarkable series of interviews with Mozart's widow, sister, and sister-in-law is in A Mozart Pilgrimage: Being the Travel Diaries of Vincent and Mary Novello in the Year 1829 (transcribed N. Medici di Marignano, ed. R. Hughes, London, 1955). The Reminiscences of the singer Michael Kelly (London, 1826; ed. R. Fiske, 1975) give a lively glimpse of Mozart; those of Lorenzo Da Ponte (Eng. translations, London and Philadelphia, 1929) are colourful but unreliable.

Biographies are many, as are studies of the music. The finest in both kinds remains Alfred Einstein's masterly study Mozart (London, 1946), even though it has been overtaken in some matters – the dating (hence the interpretation) of some works, and the author's snobbish hostility to Constanze Weber and her family. What does not date, though it is temporarily out of fashion, is Einstein's sensitivity to the music and to what it may tell us about Mozart's inner life, allied to his wide knowledge of European music and culture. One may disagree with Einstein's reading of a work and yet be enlightened by it.

Readers of this book will have gathered that in my opinion the two best-known recent biographies, W. Hildesheimer, *Mozart* (London, 1982), and Maynard Solomon, *Mozart* (London, 1995), suffer badly from over-interpretation of evidence where it exists, and over-readiness to speculate where it is lacking. Solomon's is none the less thorough and informative; Hildesheimer's is more impressionistic. Among studies that cover part of Mozart's life, H. C. Robbins Landon's *Mozart: the Golden Years* (London, 1989) and *1791: Mozart's Final Year* (London, 1988) deal in lively and enthusiastic fashion with the Vienna period – the subject also of V. Braunbehrens, *Mozart in Vienna* (London, 1990); both authors give a more industrious, workaday picture of Mozart's Viennese years than has become current through Peter Shaffer's play and film *Amadeus*.

A useful short survey of both life and works is S. Sadie's article on Mozart in *The New Grove Dictionary of Music and Musicians* (London, 1980), separately reprinted as *The New Grove Mozart* (London, 1982); a fuller, also useful collection of essays, chronologies, and catalogues of works is *The Mozart Compendium*, ed. Robbins Landon (London, 1991). More discursive essays appear in James M. Morris, ed., *On Mozart* (Cambridge, 1994).

A book that has made a big difference to the understanding of Mozart's compositional methods and to the dating of individual works is A. Tyson, *Mozart: Studies of the Autograph Scores* (Cambridge, Mass., 1987). A strong indirect light on Mozart's relation to the theatre of his time is cast by K. Honolka's life of Emanuel Schikaneder, *Papageno* (Portland, Ore., and London, 1990). Karl Barth's remarkable pages on Mozart, quoted from in the Introduction, are in his *Church Dogmatics*, ed. G. W. Bromiley and T. F. Torrance (Edinburgh, 1961, vol. III, part 3, pp. 297–9).

On Mozart's Freemasonry and his political attitudes in general, the best of the studies favouring a radical interpretation is G. Knepler, *Wolfgang Amadé Mozart* (Cambridge, 1993). A counterblast comes in Derek Beales's lecture *Mozart and the Habsburgs* (University of Reading, 1993). Beales's life of Joseph II (vol. I, Cambridge, 1987) is the outstanding historical study of the period; vol. II, when it comes, will deal with the years 1780–90, those of Mozart's Viennese career. E. Wangermann, *The Austrian Achievement* (London, 1973), provides a useful short account.

The most penetrating study of the music, along with Einstein's, is

Charles Rosen, *The Classical Style* (London, 1971); it does not, however, set out to be comprehensive. There are studies of *Mozart's Operas* by D. Heartz (Berkeley, 1990) and by E. J. Dent (2nd edn, Oxford, 1947), of *The Mozart–Da Ponte Operas* by A. Steptoe (Oxford, 1988), of *Mozart's Symphonies* by N. Zaslaw (London, 1989); *A Companion to Mozart's Piano Concertos* by A. Hutchings (Oxford, 2nd edn, 1950) needs to be supplemented by Joseph Kerman's penetrating essay in Morris, ed., *On Mozart* (see above).

For individual operas, much of the best history and criticism is in the series of Cambridge Opera Handbooks: those on *Idomeneo* (1993) and *Don Giovanni* (1981) by J. Rushton (with, in the latter volume, an essay by Bernard Williams on 'Don Giovanni as an idea'), on *The Abduction from the Seraglio* (1987) by T. Bauman, on *The Marriage of Figaro* (1987) by T. Carter, on *Così fan tutte* (1995) by Bruce Alan Brown, on *La clemenza di Tito* (1991) by J. A. Rice, on *The Magic Flute* (1991) by P. Branscombe (with an essay on the music by Erik Smith). Rushton's two volumes in particular stand out.

Recordings of Mozart's music are so many that it would be pointless to give detailed advice. Certain conductors have mastered (not necessarily in every recording) a buoyancy and pace vital to the performance of that music: Fritz Busch, Thomas Beecham, Erich Kleiber, Vittorio Gui, Karl Böhm, George Szell, Colin Davis, John Eliot Gardiner, Riccardo Muti, Jeffrey Tate, and no doubt others. Murray Perahia's complete recording of the piano concertos with the English Chamber Orchestra has made a lasting difference to understanding of those works, without putting in the shade other greatly gifted pianists who have recorded them.

Performances on period instruments may vary greatly in what they convey as practice approximating to that of Mozart's day. Gardiner's recordings, for instance – so far of operas, church works, and piano concertos (with a fortepiano soloist) – are strong on pace (not necessarily headlong) but keep to an orchestral sound smoother than one gets in, say, Christopher Hogwood's account of the complete symphonies. In yet other recordings the string bowing seems to lean on nearly every note. How far any of these reproduces what Mozart's contemporaries heard is at once a point for controversy among specialists and ultimately unknowable. At all events the use of period instruments thins and clarifies the sound in comparison with that produced by modern symphony orchestras. Listeners could to worse than experiment with various kinds of interpretation and then trust their own response.

The Italian comic operas benefit from Italian singers but often do not get them; when that happens, the recitative suffers, a particular problem in *Così fan tutte*. Non-Italian women singers have often done better than men in mastering the language: Sena Jurinac, Suzanne Danco, Nan Merriman, Lisa della Casa, Elisabeth Söderström (with Thomas Allen a laudable exception among the men). The German operas fare better in attracting native singers. On the whole, the person who does most to determine the value of a Mozart opera recording is the conductor.